Introducing the Cultural Context of the New Testament

John J. Pilch, Ph.D.

HEAR THE WORD!
Volume 2

PAULIST PRESS

New York/Mahwah

Published by Paulist Press
997 Macarthur Boulevard
Mahwah, NJ 07430

Printed and bound in the
United States of America

CONTENTS

Introduction

Father Isaac Thomas Hecker (1819–1888), founder of the
Paulist Fathers, said: "I have the conviction that I can be
all the better Catholic because I am an American; and all
the better American because I am Catholic." The Paulist
Press is just one of the ministries developed by the followers of Father Hecker to help all American Catholics fulfill
that conviction.

Father Hecker's conviction anticipated the Second Vatican Council by nearly one hundred years. In their Pastoral
Constitution on the Church in the Modern World, the council fathers observed:

> Faithful to her own tradition and at the same
> time conscious of her universal mission, [the
> Church] can enter into communion with vari-
> ous cultural modes, to her own enrichment and
> theirs too. (no. 58)

This is as true of the twentieth-century United States as it
is of any contemporary third world country.

American Catholics should be encouraged to strive
for a deeper understanding of their culture and their
faith. But such an effort soon discovers that American
culture and the culture of our biblical ancestors in the
faith are quite different from each other. If the differences between these two cultures are not recognized and

respected, the modern American Bible reader unwittingly transforms the persons of the Bible into Americans. Biblical characters begin to look, think, speak and behave like Americans. From this perspective, interpreting the Bible is easy because the English words, phrases and sentences we read in our translations are presumed to mean exactly what we understand by these same words.

Our ancestors, however, spoke a different language (Hebrew, Aramaic, Greek and perhaps others) and lived in a different culture. To be considerate readers and show respect to our ancestors it would be helpful to understand that culture.

This Bible-study program adopts such an approach as a complement to the many fine Bible programs, handbooks, and resources currently available. It will not repeat what can be easily found in other reliable sources, but will seek to understand the cultural context in which our ancestors lived.

At the same time, the new challenge resulting from such a study will be the need for a redoubled effort to make appropriate applications to our lives. After all, we are Americans and not Mediterraneans. Our cultures are different. Their problems are not our problems; their solutions might not work for us. This is why the American bishops caution us against trying "to find in the Bible all the direct answers for living."

Bridging our different cultures is possible, but it requires serious study and skilled efforts. This program hopes to assist in every way it can.

Father Hecker also noted:

> So far as it is compatible with faith and piety, I am accepting the American civilization with its usages and customs; leaving aside other reasons, it is the only way by which Catholicity can become the religion of our people. The character and spirit of our people, and of their institutions, must find themselves at home in our Church in the way those of other nations have

done; and it is on this basis alone that the Catholic religion can make progress in our country.

To know American culture well will make us better Americans. To understand the Mediterranean culture of our biblical ancestors in the faith will help us appreciate our Catholic identity. Developing a creative link between the two cultures will help us to realize Father Hecker's dream. It is a dream shared not only by his followers, the Paulists, but one worthy to be shared by all American Catholics as well.

How to Use This Workbook

This workbook is designed for any adult who is interested in a serious and/or scientific study of the Bible. It is a workbook in the sense that few Bible passages are quoted; the reader must find and read these passages in a Bible. After reading the biblical passage in its context, the reader is invited to write out the full text, or jot down notes, or mark up a personal copy of the Bible and, of course, to answer the questions in this workbook that are keyed to what was just read.

> This Bible-study program therefore requires only a few things:
> 1. A Bible
> 2. This workbook
> 3. Sufficient time to read the Bible, use the workbook, and reflect individually or discuss with others.

For those interested in pursuing some of the insights and topics further, other resources are listed. *These are not required as part of this program, nor is it expected that anyone will have the time to consult these resources while studying this program.* The references are provided as an answer to the anticipated question from some participants: "What next?" Or "Where can I read more about this?"

Serious or scientific study of the Bible is not the same as meditating on the Bible, or praying with the Bible, or reading the Bible for pleasure. All of these are legitimate uses of the Bible, and Bible study will contribute to all of them. Serious or scientific study of the Bible is just like any other such study you have already experienced in life, whether the field was business, health care, or learning a craft or skill like typing, playing a musical instrument, or computer processing. A number of things are involved.

1. Time. Serious study takes time. How much time will this study take: an hour? two? more? That depends on many things, such as how much the learner already knows, how fast the learner can search for and find the passages in the Bible, and how quickly any individual can grasp and apply new ideas and strategies. Above all, it depends on how much time is available, or how much time one can make available. Learners, individually and as a group, will have to determine how to arrange the time advantageously.

Under ideal conditions, this program would envisage a couple of hours in preparation; perhaps two or three hours for the lesson itself; and a couple of hours as follow-up. The ideal minimum amount of time for each topic thus would be six hours. Obviously, these six hours are spread out over a few days or a week and are not expected to be devoted to the session at a single sitting.

How should the eight topics in each book be studied—over a period of eight weeks or eight months? A group in Memphis, Tennessee using a highly successful Adult Bible study program published by Paulist Press met once a week for eight weeks.

BUT that program expected that the participants had been studying daily for five days, had reviewed and reflected upon that study on the sixth day, and then met on the seventh day in a small group in order to share insights. This is one form of a once-a-week meeting that extends over eight weeks. Obviously, much more time is involved than the formula "two hours once a week for eight weeks" indicates.

Hear the Word! proposes a similar time commitment. If the learner decides on once a week, that period will gain in value from some preparation and from some follow-up. At an earlier time of life these were called "preparing for class" and "homework," respectively. Anyone who took those activities seriously remembers that they paid rich dividends then. They still can now.

2. Commitment. In the tiny village of Grouard, 230 miles northwest of Edmonton, in the province of Alberta in Canada, a small group of people explored the feasibility of initiating a weekly program of Bible study. Even in this small town, activities filled almost every evening and made it difficult for the Bible-study group to select a time convenient for everyone.

However, knowledge of the Bible was a requisite in a locally-based Ministry-Formation program, and participants in this Bible-study program each "invested" a significant sum of money to purchase the materials. These two elements (a requirement and an "investment") seemed to strengthen the group members' commitment to the perfect attendance that followed. In fairness it must also be noted that the participants discovered that they actually enjoyed serious study of the Bible. And their joy was so contagious that, within a year, two new groups formed, and the busy village managed to clear Monday nights on the calendar, so that the Bible-study groups could meet without distractions from other events.

Whatever your motive for devoting yourself to serious study of the Bible, strive for strong commitment. This is as important for the lone learner as it is for the learner who is a member of a group. Once the time has been established, resolve not to miss any part of it except for the most serious of reasons.

3. Participation. Like many other programs, the success of this one, too, depends upon participation. Basically, in this program participation means *reading*! The learner must read the Bible and read the workbook. It is imperative to look up all the Bible texts suggested and to read them in the light of the information and strategies suggested in the workbook.

It is helpful if a learner has at least one partner with whom to discuss and share what is being learned. It is preferable to participate in a small group which allows for the interplay of a variety of talents, experiences and insights. Moreover, with a group it is possible to divide material so that each participant is responsible for some of it but everyone will gain in the communal meeting and sharing.

The knowledge gained in this program will not only enhance personal knowledge of the Bible and its Mediterranean cultural context but will also heighten the learner's awareness of the need for similar cultural sensitivity in comprehending news items reported from around the globe. Understanding and respecting foreign cultures are not strong suits in American culture.

The Method

Each session or chapter in the book contains three parts: Preparation; Lesson; Follow-up.

Preparation. The purpose of the preparation is to stimulate or awaken the desire to learn. A variety of strategies are invoked. Pertinent films available on videocassette offer unique challenges. Even if the films are unavailable, or time for viewing films is scarce, references are made at least to key scenes as they relate to the lesson at hand.

More than 58 percent of homes in the United States have a videocassette recorder, and practically every institution has one for its educational programs. A good picture is worth a thousand words, and there are many excellent "pictures" that can make the points of this Bible-study program quickly and effectively.

At other times, summaries of research are proposed as a framework for reading texts. Whatever stimulates interest in the topic at hand is acceptable. Alternatives—especially films or other audio-visual aids—discovered by the readers themselves would be welcome additions. Experience indicates that once learners discover an exciting insight, they are able to locate many excellent illustrations of the insight.

Lesson. This is, of course, the heart of the program. This is what the learner is expected to master. It is expected that the learner will read all biblical passages and will explore and analyze them in the cultural context presented. Discussion with others is especially helpful, but a solo learner can also manage well. Even so, don't hesitate to tailor the material to suit the time available.

Follow-up. No amount of time allotted for the lesson is ever enough. It is wise to set limits and to stick with the time limit established. The follow-up suggestions are intended to help the learner utilize some time after the lesson either to continue the lesson, or to "follow-up" its insights with additional explorations or investigations.

Logistically, the learner or the group will have to determine how to arrange time so that the follow-up does not impinge on the preparation for the next session.

The Individual Learner

The person who is unable to join in a group venture can still benefit from this program. Obviously, the major benefit is that the time which might have been spent in discussions and meetings with other learners can now be devoted to reading, especially the Bible.

On the other hand, the disadvantage for the solo learner is the lost opportunity to hear other interpretations and viewpoints as well as the definite loss of enhanced effectiveness and efficient use of scarce time that derives from group collaboration on a common project.

The individual learner, therefore, should seek opportunities for sharing knowledge even in the most informal settings. The opportunity to summarize and report to others what one has learned is a valuable motivating factor for mastering what one is learning. Such sharing might also interest the listener in taking up a similar program of serious Bible study.

Session One

"How Do You Read?"

As you read this book or any printed material, for that matter, have you ever reflected on your priceless talent: the ability to read?

The United Nations Educational, Social, and Cultural Organization (UNESCO) has noted that 25 percent of the world's adults are illiterate!

The United States Department of Education, Adult Literacy Program, recognizes that about 13 percent of Americans who are twenty years old and older can be considered functionally illiterate. The basic skills of a person who is functionally illiterate do not reach beyond the fourth grade.

In the ancient Mediterranean world, the picture was even worse. Very likely 90 percent of the population of first-century Palestine were peasants. Only 10 percent were the elite. The number in either group that could read was rather limited. That Jesus could read the Torah scroll in the synagogue singled him out as an exceptional person (see Luke 4:16).

In his ministry, as recorded in the gospels, Jesus is careful to discriminate between those who can read and those not likely to possess that skill.

During the sermon on the mount, and very often

throughout his ministry, Jesus repeatedly addresses his predominantly peasant audience with this reminder: "You have *heard* it said..." (Matthew 5:21–48). Unable to read, they have learned what they needed to know by listening to those who could read, such as the scribes, Pharisees, Sadducees, chief priests, elders and the like. Indeed, when addressing these latter groups, Jesus repeatedly asks: "Have you not *read*?" (Matthew 12:3, Mark 2:25, Luke 6:3).

This lesson will focus on the process of *reading*. It will pay special attention to how we modern Americans read ancient texts. It will invite you to reflect upon what a person does when reading texts.

Preparation: Reading: ideas or scenarios?

Lesson: Scenarios from Mediterranean culture

Follow-up: Testing another scenario

PREPARATION

Pause to consider what takes place as you read.

Ideas

Some scholars claim that when a person reads, the text generates ideas in the reader's mind. So any text that is read and understood communicates ideas which a reader should be able to comprehend and understand.

READ Matthew 5:13–18.

What ideas does this passage generate in your mind?

What kind of interpretations of this passage have you "read" or "heard" prior to this present time?

What do you think that Matthew's Jesus intended to say to his first-century Palestinian audience when he suggested that his followers are or should be like "salt" or like a "lit lamp"?

What do you think Jesus' audience understood when they heard the exhortation in these verses?

What kind of "ideas" would they have had?

Scenarios

Other specialists in reading claim that whenever an author writes, that author selects a segment of human behavior, and presents it in a language known by the author and the reader. The reader brings her or his full knowledge of culture and society to this written segment, a piece of language, and allows the author to "manipulate" the reader's knowledge so that it will match the author's vision.

Imagine (and draw, if you like) the following cartoon: Two well-known comic strip characters, Frank and Ernest, stand facing each other on a rocky and barren terrain while each one leans on a long-handled shovel. In the background are the ruins of ancient buildings. Frank says to Ernest: "I've been an archeologist for thirty-seven years. Nobody knows the rubbles I've seen."

Because the actual cartoon is not reproduced here, a reader has to imagine the scenario.

What does the rocky terrain look like?

Is the sun shining or are the skies overcast?

How are Frank and Ernest dressed?

What nationality are Frank and Ernest?

Are they digging in their native country, or another country?

What is the purpose of their digging?

Finally, what is the significance of Frank's statement?

Does that statement remind you of anything?

Does the statement resemble the lyrics from a song?

Does this cartoon have anything to do with slavery in the United States?

Finally, how much information do you have to bring to this text in order to construct a complete scenario for this one-frame cartoon?

Where did you draw this information from?

Where did you gather the mental pictures you formed as you imagined this comic strip?

If this all sounds like a silly exercise, READ Matthew 13:44. How have you previously imagined this parable of the treasure hidden in the field?

Does it make much difference that the "Frank and Ernest" comic strip appears in an American newspaper, while the gospel story originated in the Mediterranean world?

Comic strips are an example of "high context" literature, just as legal contracts or credit card-agreements are examples of "low context" literature. Low context literature leaves next to nothing to the reader's imagination; all details are spelled out. This is why the context is described as low.

High context literature presumes that the reader will supply the appropriate details. Much poetry is high context literature. The Japanese poem form known as a "haiku" is one example. The Bible in general is another example of high context literature, for it provides precious few of the details of Mediterranean culture that the author expects a considerate reader to apply to the proper understanding of the text.

Reading specialists point out that readers bring to high context texts *scenarios* from the social world and the social system that they know. Americans will naturally imagine and supply the American social world and social system to the Mediterranean texts they read, because they read these ancient texts in English translation.

In the lesson to follow, we will observe how inappropriate are the scenarios we bring from our American culture to ancient Mediterranean texts. We will then encourage readers to learn and to master Mediterranean scenarios in order to become respectful readers of the New Testament, and indeed, of the entire Bible.

LESSON: Words and Language: "Salt of the Earth"

The Greek word for "earth" in the New Testament most likely translates a Hebrew and Aramaic word that has two meanings: "earth" and "earth-oven."

Jesus' exhortation to his disciples that they should be "salt" makes best Mediterranean, literal, cultural sense when the phrase is "earth-oven" rather than "earth." So Matthew's Jesus has urged: "You (his followers in general) should be salt for the earth-oven."

In first-century Palestine, ovens were made from earth or clay. They are similar to the familiar "*horno*" which one can still see on the reservations of New Mexico.

The fuel burned in this earth-oven was camel and donkey dung. As a part of growing up, young girls were trained to collect and roll this animal dung into patties. Then it was salted and left to dry in the sun. This dried animal dung was subsequently burned as needed in the earth-oven.

The floor of the oven was lined with a flat plate or block of salt which served as a catalyst for burning the fuel. Salt has the capacity to make things burn.

READ Psalm 12:6.

What are the words of the Lord compared to?

Where is this silver refined?

The Hebrew literally reads: "in a furnace [made] of earth." How does your version translate this phrase?

READ Job 28:5.

Where does bread come from—the earth, or an earth-oven?

What is ravaged by fire—the earth, or earth-oven?

This is the *scenario* Matthew and the other evangelists can reliably expect their Mediterranean readers to bring to the gospel texts, so that each respective author can manipulate the scenario in the reader's mind in order to communicate to that considerate reader.

Salt thus placed on the oven floor and salt sprinkled on the dung serves as a catalyst helping the fuel to burn. After a few years, the heat of the fire causes the salt crystals of the oven to undergo a chemical reaction. As a result, the salt now impedes and stifles the burning of the dung. It is when these crystals are thus transformed chemically that the salt loses its "saltiness," or catalytic ability. Salt, of course, never loses its salty taste, but who would want to taste salt on which dung has been laid?

Please bring this Mediterranean cultural scenario along as you read the New Testament "salt" passages.

READ Matthew 5:13.

Should the follower of Jesus be a seasoning? a preservative? or a catalyst?

Does salt ever lose its "saltiness"?

Does a catalyst ever lose its catalytic ability?

What does one do with the salt plate or block that one removes from the oven—use it for flavoring, for preserving, or a solid footing in a muddy path?

Using these verses as the conclusion to his version of the beatitudes, what point does Matthew want Jesus to make?

READ Mark 9:49–50.

Jesus has just spoken about scandal (v 42), that is, about causing those who believe in him to sin. Then he urges that a person should get rid of the instrument of scandal at all costs in order to avoid being thrown into hell "where the fire never dies out" (v 48).

The word "fire" quite naturally brings to mind the

catalyst: salt! Hence the logical sequence from verse 48 to verses 49 and 50.

What does it mean "to be salted for the fire?"

Is it similar to the dung which is thus prepared to be fuel in the earth-oven?

Does "salted for the fire" have anything to do with "being a catalyst"?

Salt is indeed good, but if it loses catalytic ability, then what?

Why would Jesus urge his listeners "to be salty" but at the same time "to stay at peace with one another"?

Is it possible that a salty person, a catalyst, stirs up trouble, or starts fights?

READ Luke 14:34–35.

In the preceding context of these verses, Jesus urges those who would be his disciples to take stock before beginning a project lest they be shamed by their inability to complete it. He uses the example of planning for a war. And his concluding words highlight his concern: discipleship! (See verse 33.)

What impact does this last verse (Luke 14:33) have on the salt passage that follows (vv 34–35)?

What does salt/catalyst have to do with discipleship?

Notice the literal truth of the statement: salt that has lost catalytic ability is good neither for the oven nor for preparing fuel. It is good neither for the land (earth, oven) nor the dunghill (potential fuel).

What is done with such salt?

What would happen to a disciple who lost catalytic ability?

READ Luke 12:49–53.

The preceding context of these verses urges that one be prepared rather than unprepared for all eventualities.

Would it be fair to say that Jesus saw his purpose as "lighting the oven" or "starting fires"? (See verse 49.)

Instead of peace, Jesus brings division (v 51). How is this "salty" characteristic played out in families as they wrestle with their estimate of Jesus? (See verses 52–53.)

RETURN AND REREAD Matthew 5.

The image of salt as a catalyst for the fire in an earth-oven leads very naturally to the next image: a lamp lit and held high for all to see.

Only this literal, Mediterranean, authentically cultural understanding of "salt" and "earth-oven" makes such a smooth combination of images in Matthew 5:13–14.

Matthew and the other evangelists counted on the listener/reader bringing a Mediterranean scenario to their texts so that they might rearrange the details of this scenario in the minds of the listener/reader and present a distinctive image of Jesus as catalyst.

For Matthew, followers of Jesus who have lost their catalytic ability for the fire, that is, have neglected, forgotten, or abandoned the "gospel," are no longer good for anything except to be "stepped on" by other people. From this perspective, persecution and insult directed to "neutralized" or "ineffective" Christians should not be understood as "persecution" for Jesus' sake.

Social Context for the Words and Language: "Salt of the Earth"

How does this fresh, Mediterranean understanding of "salt" and "oven" (or kiln) contribute to a better understanding of the Bible and its Mediterranean culture context?

Experts describe Mediterranean culture as "agonistic" or "combative." This is another way of saying that Mediterranean people in general are prone to conflict. Recall how often Jesus is involved in conflict in the gospels. Scan through the Acts of the Apostles and take note of how often the followers of Jesus find themselves in court.

This tendency toward conflict is a natural consequence of the core values of Mediterranean culture: namely, honor and shame. (Consult *Hear the Word!* Book I, Session Three: Core Cultural Values.)

Honor is a public claim to value or worth *and* public acknowledgment or affirmation of that claim. Every person in the Mediterranean world—even a beggar—is presumed to be honorable. Each person spends a lifetime guarding, protecting and maintaining that honor.

One major ongoing cultural "game" concerned with honor consists of a *challenge and response*. Individuals challenge the honorable status of their equals in the hope of catching them off guard, of putting them on the spot, so that they are unable to make an appropriate response in defense of their honor. This shames the one challenged and redounds to the honor of the one challenging.

People who play this kind of game, and that is everyone in Mediterranean culture, can certainly be called "catalytic." They love to light fires, notably the fires of conflict.

READ Mark 7:1–23.

1. All conflict begins with a grievance.

Who are the aggrieved parties? (Mark 7:1)

What is the grievance? (Mark 7:2)

If the grievance is about improper, or dishonorable, or shameful behavior (v 2), what is the proper and honorable behavior? (Mark 7:3–4)

2. The *challenge* to Jesus' honor

Who directs the challenge to Jesus? (Mark 7:5)

What is the substance of the challenge? (Mark 7:5; see also verses 3–4.)

The phrase "tradition of the elders" tells us that this behavior is not rooted in the Torah, but rather is a non-Torah tradition about "how" or "in what way" to eat.

Is it fair to conclude that these groups view Jesus and his group (disciples) as a competitive group?

Is it fair to say the competition is about "honor" or "honorable behavior"?

3. Jesus' *response* to the challenge to his (and his group's) honor

How would you interpret the words "you hypocrites" in the first sentence of Jesus' response?

Would you agree that Jesus responds to the challenge by first insulting his challengers?

What is the substance of Jesus' quotation from Isaiah 29:13? (Mark 7:6–7)

What is Jesus' *counter-challenge?* (Mark 7:8)

How does Jesus prove or support his counter-challenge? (Mark 7:9–13)

4. The *Grant of Honor*

Remember that honor is a public claim to value *and* a public acknowledgment. In this story thus far, the Pharisees and scribes have made a claim to honor, and Jesus makes a counter-claim to honor by counter-challenging his challengers.

Notice the comment in Mark 7:14. What role must "the people" play in this episode?

Doesn't the culture expect "the public" to affirm or deny the claim to honor?

How does Jesus respond to the challenge hurled at him earlier in verse 5? (See Mark 7:14–15.)

Is Jesus' response appropriate to the challenge? Compare verse 5 with verses 14–15.

Does the crowd grant honor to the challengers or to
Jesus?

If the text is not explicit on this point, what would
you hypothesize?

5. The result

Inside, apart from the crowd (Mark 7:17–23), Jesus gives
a private explanation of the "parable" or riddle he
offered as his response to the challenge. He does this regularly throughout this gospel (see Mark 4:34b).

The significance of these private explanations is that
Jesus is clearly building his own following, establishing his
own group.

In first-century Palestine, the reason why a leader
forms a group is because that leader has a grievance with
another group. The group is formed to assist that leader
in settling the grievance.

What is very clear in the gospel texts is that Jesus is
ever in conflict with other groups. The conflict in the ultimate analysis revolves about what constitutes "true honor."

For Jesus, true honor is that which God grants, and
not necessarily that which human beings confer upon one
another. And yet Jesus is involved deeply enough in his
culture that he dare not ignore the workings of honor
and shame, challenge and response, nor the cultural
necessity of being a catalyst.

Note well how absolutely fundamental to this conflict-prone society is the understanding of salt as catalyst.
Jesus' advice in Mark 9:49–50 to "remain salty" is equivalent to saying "yield no ground!", "defend your honor
when it is challenged!", "challenge the honor of and
attempt to shame or discredit other groups!"

BUT in the process, Jesus urges that people stay at peace with one another. Don't be salty with one another. Don't waste energy by challenging each other or trying to gain honor at the expense of one another, as in Mark 10:35–45 when two of the twelve in true salty fashion want more honorable places than the other ten. Focus instead on competing groups!

This is wise advice and well-considered strategy for a fledgling movement that is challenging other "traditional" and established groups.

"Peace: The Word and Its Social Context "

Everyone knows the story of David and Bathsheba (see 2 Samuel 11:2–5). After his adultery, when David learned that Bathsheba was pregnant, he summoned her husband, Uriah, from battle with the expectation that Uriah would spend the evening with his wife and thus cover up David's sin.

When Uriah arrived from the battle, David asked him literally in Hebrew about:

> the shalom of Joab;
> the shalom of the soldiers;
> and the shalom of the war (!?!?) (2 Samuel 11:7)

Shalom of the war, indeed! A recent scholarly study of the Hebrew word, *shalom*, has concluded that this simple Hebrew word has at least eight different meanings or interpretations in the Hebrew Bible! Clearly, in the passage cited, David is asking quite simply: "How is Joab? How are the soldiers? How goes it with the war?"

This passage illustrates one usage of shalom, namely, as a salutation or as a basic inquiry about something or someone.

For other examples of shalom as a salutation or a basic inquiry about something or someone, consult:

Genesis 29:6

Genesis 37:14

Genesis 43:27

1 Samuel 16:4

1 Samuel 25:6

1 Samuel 29:7

The scholarly study concluded that any presentation of "wholeness" as the radical meaning of this word (a common occurrence in the English language) is rather unjustified, given the multitudinous nuances of this rich Hebrew word.

In the New Testament, a similar caution is appropriate. Following upon our increased awareness of "salt" having the meaning of "catalyst" in New Testament literature, and our heightened appreciation of Mediterranean culture as conflict prone, at least one of the meanings of "peace" in the New Testament should be the minimalization or restriction of conflict.

And so it is!

One meaning of "peace" involves a set of favorable circumstances that includes peace and tranquility. This is a concept that stands in contrast to a psychological notion of peace as a state of mind. Americans, who tend to seek individualistic and psychological interpretation in life, need to be careful not to allow their cultural preferences to dictate or control the interpretation of New Testament texts.

READ Luke 19:41–44.

Why does Jesus weep over Jerusalem?

What does "peace" mean in verse 42?

Is peace here a circumstance or a psychological state?

READ 1 Corinthians 16:10–11.

What is Paul's concern about Timothy?

How would/should Timothy perceive a person who "despises" him? Would that be a challenge to his honor requiring a response?

What honorable behavior does Paul exhort the Corinthians to perform for Timothy?

Is peace here a circumstance or a psychological state?

A Greek adjective translated as "peaceable" describes the circumstance of tranquility and peace.

READ James 3:13–18.

How would you judge? Does the phrase "bitter jealousy and selfish ambition" describe a psychological state ("in your hearts") or a circumstance? (See James 3:14.)

For clues to the appropriate answer, consider these notions:

Where and how does one demonstrate wisdom and understanding? (See James 3:13.)

What results from "jealousy and selfish ambition"? (See James 3:16.)

What is the nature of wisdom from above? (See James 3:17.) Notice the word "peaceable" in this verse.

And finally, what condition or circumstance results from such efforts and such behavior? (See James 3:18.)

If the translation you are using has referred in James 3:18 to "peacemakers" or "those who make peace," then we have a natural opportunity to move to the consideration of a very important person in conflict-prone cultures, namely, peacemakers.

Cultures that are prone to conflict rely heavily on respected third parties to ward off potentially violent consequences of conflict. Such persons are called "mediators" or "peacemakers." Theirs is a very difficult but highly honorable task. Those who stand the best chance of success are kinspersons who are removed from the situation by at least five links! The principal function of a mediator or peacemaker is to settle blood-feuds, that is, to prevent bloodshed, death.

READ 2 Samuel 14.

When King David's son Absalom avenged the rape of his sister Tamar by murdering his rapist-brother Amnon, he fled because he had initiated a family blood-feud that required that his blood be shed.

What role did Joab assign to the Woman of Tekoa regarding the relationship of King David and his son Absalom?

Would you call her a mediator or peacemaker?

READ Matthew 5:8–9.

Beatitudes are culturally valuable lines of conduct quite obvious to anyone familiar with the workings of a culture. These paired beatitudes interpret one another and highlight culturally esteemed behaviors and roles.

In the light of our current reflection, how would you interpret "peacemaker" (v 9)?

Why is a peacemaker "God-like" (="son of God")?

For hints, consult:

Romans 15:33

Romans 16:20

1 Corinthians 7:15b

If the disciple of Jesus is supposed to be like God (READ Matthew 5:44–45, 48), and God is a God of peace, surely a "peacemaker" or "mediator" is perceived as God-like in this culture.

How do you understand "pure of heart" (v 8)?

Would such a person be one who is single-minded, who has only one thing on his mind, that is, God's righteousness as revealed in Jesus?

READ Colossians 1:15–20.

How did Jesus "make peace" in this conflict-prone society?

Did there come a time in his life when he "lost" a challenge-and-response episode?

How would you interpret his trial and execution from an honor-and-shame perspective?

What light does that shed on Colossians 1:15–20?

READ Romans 12:14–20.

In view of all that we have examined in this present lesson, how would you evaluate Paul's advice in these verses?

Does he stand a good chance of persuading people to his point of view?

How would you read this paragraph from an honor-and-shame, challenge-and-response perspective?

Is Paul asking people to give up defending honor, protecting honor, guarding honor?

Notice his advice in verse 18.

Does verse 19 offer some justification or consolation for the culturally very demanding exhortations Paul has listed until this point?

READ Luke 12:13–21.

Jesus is invited by a person to be a mediator or peacemaker (see verse 13). Does the text give any clue why Jesus refuses the invitation?

Do you notice what Jesus singles out as reprehensible here? (See verse 15.)

Is it proper, then, to conclude that the word "rich" in the gospels might more appropriately be translated "greedy"?

Could the parable offer an explanation of why Jesus declined the invitation to be a mediator?

In summary, then, peacemaker is another name for mediator, that is, any relatively distanced and disinterested third party who is highly regarded by aggrieved parties and who is skilled in the art of bringing hostile parties to a mutually honorable truce. In the agonistic Mediterranean biblical culture of our ancestors in the faith, this is a powerful and very important role.

FOLLOW-UP

"How do you read?" By now it should be evident that American Bible readers need to be very careful not to insert American scenarios into Mediterranean texts.

Here is yet another example for analysis.

READ Mark 2:23–28.

1. What behavior by the disciples stirs a grievance among opponents? (See Mark 2:23.)

2. Who is aggrieved? (See Mark 2:24.)

3. So far in this story, the events are very public; when things are so public, are honor and shame, the core cultural values, involved?

4. What, then, is the *challenge* hurled to Jesus by the aggrieved group? (See Mark 2:24.)

5. How does Jesus *respond* to the challenge? (See Mark 2:25–26.)

6. Jesus refers to an event reported in 1 Samuel 21:1–6.

   Read the passage there and carefully compare it with what Mark's Jesus has said.

7. What is the name of the high priest?

8. READ 2 Samuel 15:32–37, paying special attention to verse 35.

   What is the name of the high priest?

9. Has Jesus confused the name of the high priest at the time David ate the bread (1 Samuel 21:1–6) with the name of the high priest during David's reign as king (2 Samuel 15:35)?

10. Or do you think a better explanation is that Jesus is actually "testing" his challengers by slipping in the wrong name, feeling certain that they won't catch it, and so hoping to shame them?

11. The gospel text gives no clue about the Pharisees' response, but it seems reasonable to presume they didn't counter-challenge Jesus, either for his insult "Have you not read...?" or for his misidentification of the high priest. It also seems reasonable to assume that Jesus did not lose any disciples at this point, so his strategy for gathering and maintaining a group around him to support him in his grievance is working: he never loses in a challenge-and-response episode. Throughout the gospel, by means of these challenge and response episodes, Jesus shows that he is a capable and honorable teacher. And he does this consistently in line with the Mediterranean core cultural values.

Resources

Brown, Raymond E. *Jesus: God and Man.* Milwaukee: Bruce, 1967.

Malina, Bruce J. "A Conflict Approach to Mark 7," *Forum* 4 (3, 1988), 3–30.

Malina, Bruce J. "Why Interpret the Bible with the Social Sciences?" *American Baptist Quarterly* 2 (1983), 119–133.

Pilch, John J. "Preparing Salt for the (H)earth," *The Cate-chist's Connection*, 1 (2, October, 1984), 1–3.

Pilch, John J. "Scripture, Culture, and Catechesis," *Professional Approaches for Christian Educators (PACE)*, March, 1990.

Pilch, John J. "Stories Your Pastor Never Told You." Credence Cassettes, 1989.

Pilch. John J. "Spirituality and the Beatitudes," *The Cate-chist's Connection*, 7 (3, 1990), 1–3.

Session Two

Guidelines for Interpretation

Session one in Book One of *Hear the Word!* presented guidelines for interpreting the Bible drawn from the Vatican II Document on Divine Revelation and the United States Bishops Letter on Fundamentalism. There the focus was the Old Testament and particular examples were drawn mainly, though not exclusively, from the wisdom literature.

This present session invites the reader once more to reflect on the challenge posed to western readers in interpreting the Bible in its original, Middle-Eastern context. Here the focus is on the New Testament.

Preparation: The Declaration of Independence

Lesson: The Guidelines

Follow-up: Reflections on interpretation

PREPARATION: The Declaration of Independence

Visitors touring the monuments of Washington, D.C., invariably visit the Thomas Jefferson Memorial. Inside the Memorial building there are four panels engraved with inscriptions based on the writings of Jefferson.

More than anything else, Jefferson wanted to be remembered as the author of the Declaration of Independence. A selection from the Declaration is located on the southwestern wall panel. In the columns below, compare the inscription on the wall with the actual final text preserved in the National Archives.

WALL INSCRIPTION	FINAL TEXT—ARCHIVES
WE HOLD THESE TRUTHS TO BE SELF-EVIDENT:	We hold these truths to be self-evident,
THAT ALL MEN ARE CREATED EQUAL,	that all men are created equal,
THAT THEY ARE ENDOWED BY THEIR CREATOR WITH CERTAIN INALIENABLE RIGHTS,	that they are endowed by their Creator with certain unalienable rights,
AMONG THESE ARE LIFE, LIBERTY, AND THE PURSUIT OF HAPPINESS.	that among these are life, liberty and the pursuit of happiness.
THAT TO SECURE THESE RIGHTS GOVERNMENTS ARE INSTITUTED AMONG MEN.	That to secure these rights, governments are instituted among men, deriving....
WE ... SOLEMNLY PUBLISH AND DECLARE,	We ... solemnly publish and declare,

THAT THESE COLONIES ARE AND OF RIGHT OUGHT TO BE FREE AND INDEPENDENT STATES . . .	That these United Colonies are, and of right ought to be Free and Independent States; . . .
AND FOR THE SUPPORT OF THIS DECLARATION, WITH A FIRM RELIANCE ON THE PROTECTION OF DIVINE PROVIDENCE,	And for the support of this declaration, with a firm reliance on the protection of Divine Providence,
WE MUTUALLY PLEDGE OUR LIVES, OUR FORTUNES, AND OUR SACRED HONOUR.	we mutually pledge to each other our lives, our fortunes, and our sacred honor.

The wall inscription is carved in capital letters as in column one above, but if you have a keen eye, you will still have noted *eleven errors* which have been identified by scholars in this inscription:

in three places, Jefferson's words are omitted;

in six places, there are punctuation errors;

two of Jefferson's words are misspelled.

The spellings "inalienable" and "honour" are indeed found in Jefferson's rough draft but not in the final version. Some speculate that the architects may have thought they were being particularly scholarly in using the earlier spellings.

The punctuation errors and omission of words appear to have a much simpler explanation. The Thomas Jefferson Memorial Commission created by Congress in 1934 apparently gave permission to the architects Otto R. Eggers and Daniel P. Higgins to omit words and punctuation which these architects claimed were necessary in order to save space!

These omissions allowed the excerpt on the Memorial wall to be carefully laid out so that the right margin is justified or squared, an eye-pleasing effect which a faithful reproduction of Jefferson's text would have made impossible.

The Thomas Jefferson Memorial was dedicated on April 13, 1943.

What do you know about the efforts of Jefferson in writing this Declaration of Independence?

Was he painstaking in choosing words?

Did he encounter any objections to the document he drew up among the members of the Second Continental Congress who in June, 1776, accepted Virginia representative Richard Henry Lee's resolution "that these United Colonies are, and of right ought to be, free and independent states"?

Was Jefferson's modified document accepted unanimously by the Second Continental Congress?

Do you think the Memorial Commission acted properly in permitting Jefferson's text to be altered so that it could be neatly inscribed on the southwest wall of the Memorial?

Does it make any difference that the sense of the Declaration does not seem to be changed by the "errors" on the inscription?

Is it important to consider and respect the intentions of Jefferson and the Continental Congress?

Is the Declaration of Independence anything like a "sacred text" for Americans?

Who interprets the Declaration of Independence?

Are there any principles or guidelines for interpreting the Declaration of Independence?

How do you think Jefferson or the members of the Second Continental Congress might have responded to the changes "approved" by the Memorial Commission?

Reflecting upon and discussing this American example of interpretation is especially important for this Bible-study program. Americans in general who place a high value on individualism place a correspondingly high value on individual (also called personal or private) interpretation. The same autonomy which Americans claim for themselves in interpreting their civic documents they extend also to other documents like papal pronouncements and the Bible. "Nobody tells me what to think or do!" is a fair summary of the American attitude.

The church encourages its members to read the Bible and realizes that all reading involves interpretation. The church, therefore, provides guidelines for interpreting texts, and it is to these guidelines that we now turn our attention in order to learn how to respect the mind and intentions of the original authors much as we presumably hope to respect the mind and intentions of our country's founding fathers, such as Thomas Jefferson.

LESSON

Some guidelines provided by the church to assist readers in the interpretation of the New Testament are found in the following documents:

> The Historical Truth of the Gospels (The 1964 Instruction of the Biblical Commission)
>
> The Vatican II Dogmatic Constitution on Divine Revelation (1965), especially Chapters III and V.
>
> The 1987 Pastoral Statement for Catholics by the U.S. Bishops on Biblical Fundamentalism.

In Book One of *Hear the Word!* we examined portions of these documents in the sequence in which they were written, with biblical examples presented to illustrate the specific guidelines. Here we shall focus instead on a specific biblical text, The Parable of the Vineyard Workers, and draw appropriate passages from these documents to illustrate how they guide an interpreter in dealing with a concrete, specific passage of the New Testament.

READ Matthew 20:1–16.

I. A Parable

The text of Matthew does not explicitly call this story a parable. The phrase, "The reign of God is like," however, clearly indicates that this is indeed a parable. The British scholar, Charles H. Dodd, phrased the classic definition of the parable:

> At its simplest the parable is a metaphor or simile drawn from nature or common life, arresting the hearer by its vividness or strangeness, and leaving the mind in sufficient doubt about its precise application to tease it into active thought. (*The Parables of the Kingdom*. London: Nisbet & Co., 1936, p. 16)

Church Guidelines

"When the Lord was orally explaining his doctrine, He followed the modes of reasoning and of exposition which were in vogue at the time." (Historical Truth, VII)

What elements of this parable reveal it to be a very fitting "mode of exposition" in vogue at the time of Jesus? Look for the elements of a parable highlighted by Dodd in Matthew's verses and record them below.

Is this a metaphor or simile?

Does this reflect nature or common life?

What elements display vividness?

What elements strike you as strange?

Does this parable arrest a listener, or can a listener let it in one ear and out the other?

What might have struck the original listeners as strange?

Is the application clear, or is the listener left in sufficient doubt so as to be motivated to think further about the parable?

"Christ established the Kingdom of God on earth, manifested His Father and Himself by deeds and words, and completed His work by His death, resurrection, and glorious ascension and by the sending of the Holy Spirit." (Vatican II on Revelation, n. 17)

Is it fair to describe a parable as one category of "words" by which Christ manifested his Father and himself?

On the basis of your current knowledge of the Bible, what do Christ's words in this parable manifest about his Father or himself?

"Holy Mother Church has firmly and with absolute constancy held, and continues to hold, that the four Gospels just stated, whose historical character the Church unhesitatingly asserts, faithfully hand on what Jesus Christ, while living among men, really did and taught for their eternal salvation, until the day He was taken up into heaven (see Acts 1:1–2)." (Vatican II on Revelation, n. 19)

How do you interpret the phrase "historical character"? Would this phrase mean that Jesus "really" spoke this parable?

Does "historical character" mean that the topic of this parable really happened?

Could "historical character" mean that the parable's story line is culturally plausible?

Modern biblical scholars are agreed that Matthew 20:1–15 was truly and authentically spoken by Jesus.

"Those who search out the intention of the sacred writers must, among other things, have regard for 'literary forms.' For truth is proposed and expressed in a variety of ways, depending on whether a text is history of one kind or another, or whether its form is that of prophecy, poetry, or some other kind of speech." (Vatican II on Revelation, n. 12)

> Would you consider the parable a "literary form" according to this quotation?

As Jesus "spoke" parables, they of course would not be "literary" forms; but as the evangelists recorded parables in their gospels, they do become "literary" forms. The significance of this distinction will become clear later in this session, especially relative to the concluding verses of the parable.

II. Three Layers of Tradition in the Gospels

The Biblical Commission instruction on the Historicity of the Gospels urges that "the interpreter should pay diligent attention to the three stages of tradition by which the doctrine and life of Jesus have come down to us." (Instruction, VI)

Stage One: What Jesus said and did. (Instruction n. VII)

> Jesus himself selected disciples who witnessed and understood what he said and did.

Jesus followed the modes of reasoning and of exposition which were in vogue at the time.

Stage Two: What the apostles proclaimed about what Jesus said and did. (Instruction n. VIII)

The apostles passed on to their listeners what Jesus really said and did but with that fuller understanding which they enjoyed.

Moreover, they too interpreted his words and deeds according to the needs of their listeners.

They used various modes of speaking suited to their own purpose and the mentality of their listeners: catecheses, stories, testimonial, hymns, doxologies, prayers and other literary forms.

Stage Three: What the evangelists selected, reduced to a synthesis, or further explicated from what the apostles preached about what Jesus really said and did. (Instruction n. IX)

Pay attention to the sequence in which the various evangelists pass on the words and deeds of the savior; context is important.

The evangelists often express Jesus' sayings, not literally, but differently, while preserving their sense.

The Commission concludes this section by noting that unless the interpreter pays attention to *all* these things, it is impossible to fulfill the task of probing into what the sacred writers intended and what they really said. (Instruction n. X)

Have you ever read or heard about these three layers of tradition contained in the gospels?

Do the preachers you hear relate these layers in their homilies?

Do you know how these layers or stages of tradition are discerned and identified?

Jesus:

How and where can a person learn the "modes of reasoning and of exposition" current at the time of Jesus?

Do you think Jesus was an authentic native of Mediterranean culture who reasoned and spoke like other Mediterranean natives?

To be even more specific, Jesus was an artisan. Where can you learn more about Mediterranean artisans of the ancient world?

Can you think of any modern Mediterranean cultures which have remained virtually unchanged for thousands of years?

Would Jesus be more like the people of these cultures, or more like Americans?

The Apostles:

How did the apostles gain a "fuller understanding" of what Jesus said and did?

How can a reader discern the "interpretation" which these apostles gave to Jesus' words and deeds?

How can a reader learn more about the "needs" of those who listened to the apostles?

Can these "needs" be deduced from the texts we have?

The Evangelists:

The gospel text in translation available to a modern reader represents the "final product" of the efforts of an evangelist on the preaching of the apostles about their memories of what Jesus said and did.

Have you ever attempted to sort out the three layers of tradition in this final text?

In the illustration that follows, we shall work jointly on that process.

III. Identifying the Layers of Tradition in the Vineyard Workers Parable

One way of investigating a gospel parable is to look carefully at the ending and then ask if it makes a sensible conclusion to the story.

Consider the "endings" to this parable:

(1) Matthew 20:16b: "Many are called but few are chosen."

Does your Bible contain this verse?

Catholic translations from the Latin Vulgate, such as the Challoner-Rheims (e.g., the old CCD translation) used to have this verse, but translations based on critically edited Greek texts (e.g., the Kleist-Lilly translation) did not have it. The new New Testament of the *New American Bible* published in 1986 does not report this verse. The reason for omitting it is based on ancient manuscript evidence. The most reliable and oldest (fourth and fifth centuries) Greek manuscripts known to scholars simply do not contain the passage. It was added at a later time, most likely by scribes. It is properly omitted here, though Matthew 22:14 does use this saying to conclude a different story.

> Which layer of tradition could this verse represent—Jesus? the apostolic preachers? the evangelists? Be bold and adventuresome in your thinking. The answer(s) may not be all that simple.

(2) Matthew 20:16a: "First will be last, and the last first."

Does this verse make a sensible ending to the story?

If the first hired were paid first, would they stick around to see what the last hired were paid?

If the first hired did not know what the last hired were paid, would the last hired tell them?

If the first hired were paid first, and didn't stick around, and didn't find out what the last hired were paid, would the story collapse? Who would grumble?

Could Jesus, the masterful storyteller, have told a story with an ending that does not seem to be appropriate?

Which layer of tradition could this verse represent—Jesus? the apostolic preachers? the evangelist? For a clue, READ Matthew 19:30.

Does this verse look familiar?

If a reader were to write out Matthew 19:30 in a straight line, and directly beneath it Matthew 20:16a, a pattern would become visible:

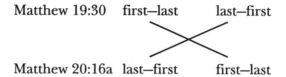

Matthew 19:30   first—last   last—first

Matthew 20:16a last—first   first—last

Draw a line from one pair of words in the first line to its corresponding pair of words in the second line.

What letter of the alphabet do the lines create?

Does the letter look like an "X"?

In Greek, this letter "X" is called "chi," and the literary pattern or device formed by such corresponding phrases or sentences is called a "chiasm." The verses (19:30 and 20:16) are like two pieces of bread intended to "sandwich" the unit between them, or like the floors of a building supported by crisscrossed beams.

Only Matthew tells this story about the vineyard workers. Scholars are agreed that it is original with Jesus, but ancient authors do not seem to have remembered its original life-setting. Matthew did not want to omit the story, yet had to find a new setting for it in his gospel. So at the end of the story of Jesus' promised reward to the Twelve, the concluding verse (19:30) suggested to Matthew that he could insert the vineyard workers story here. When he had finished the vineyard workers story, he repeated the verse of 19:30 in order to indicate this episode was ended, and his gospel story line would continue.

In the light of this reflection, which layer of tradition does Matthew 20:16 represent—Jesus? the apostolic preachers? or the evangelist?

(3) READ Matthew 20:15: envy of generosity.

Shouldn't an owner have the right to determine how to handle his own business?

Does this make a sensible ending to the story?

Do you like this ending?

Do you agree with this ending?

Does this ending "leave in the mind sufficient doubt" about the precise meaning of the parable so as to tease a person to think more about it?

Would any additional information be useful for a proper and satisfactory interpretation of this story?

IV. The Mediterranean Cultural Dimension of the Vineyard Workers Parable

The worst scenario (recall session one in this book) that a modern western reader could bring to this text is that of American job-hunting, labor unions, contracts, fair wages and the like. Economics as it is known in the western world simply did not exist in the ancient Mediterranean world. People "made a living" in that place and at that time in a rather different but very successful way. Here are a few items that are in the biblical text but which remain invisible to western eyes until and unless they are called to a reader's attention.

A. The World of Limited Good

READ Matthew 20:3–7.

Did the idle workers apply for a job?

Did the vineyard owner go out and hire every idle worker without any of them asking for a job?

Does it strike you as strange in verse 7 that the idle workers "stand here idle all day" because no one hired (or asked, or invited) them?

In the ancient Mediterranean world, it was firmly believed that all available goods were finite in number and already distributed. The consequence of this belief is: "There is no more where this came from."

The vineyard owner possessed a valuable good. Its

annual crop was valuable, and it was all his. If he were to lose the crop, that loss would be tragic indeed. It would certainly be similar to the tragic loss of a coin by the woman who had ten (see Luke 15:8–9). In each and every case, "there is no more where this came from."

If an unemployed worker came to the vineyard owner and asked for a job, that action would be a presumption and imposition in a limited-good culture. It would be equivalent to trying to get something (some of the harvest, or a wage) to which the unemployed worker is not at all entitled. Asking for a job in this context is shameful, but not because of unemployment, as in our culture. Rather, the shame is in actually being bold enough to think that the vineyard owner for some reason "owes" the petitioner a job! The honorable behavior for an unemployed person in the ancient Mediterranean culture is to stand around and wait to be asked or invited to work.

In this story, the vineyard owner goes out five times and invites idle workers to join his labor force. That is honorable behavior for him, and being asked rather than asking for a job is honorable behavior for the idle workers. In a society which believes that all goods are limited, people are very careful not to make a claim to something to which they have no claim.

B. "The Evil Eye" = Jealousy

READ Matthew 20:15.

How does your translation present this sentence?

A literal translation of the Greek text is: "Is your eye evil because I am good?" Belief in "the evil eye" is a truly crosscultural phenomenon appearing in approximately sixty-seven cultures of the world, or approximately thirty-seven percent of the total world sample in a classic study of world cultures. Its origins have been traced to the ancient Near East, India, and cultures surrounding the Mediterranean Sea.

Essentially, these cultures believe that some people, animals, demons or gods have a power to cast spells or cause a bad effect on every object upon which their eye or glance may rest. This glance can work involuntarily, but most often it is intentional. The glance is associated with envy and greed, stinginess and covetousness, and is directed against objects which displease the viewer. The phrase "evil eye" found in the Greek New Testament is usually rendered in English translations as "envy" or "jealousy."

Note well: In Mediterranean culture, envy (or the evil eye) implies a wish to steal that specific item from the owner or to cause the owner to lose that specific item in some way. In mainstream U.S. culture, envy describes the wish on the part of one person to have an item just like the one another person possesses, but not that very same item. Neither does the mainstream U.S. idea of envy include the wish to deprive the envied person of the goods which are envied or to destroy them.

In this story of the vineyard workers, the complaint of the first-hired workers to the vineyard owner prompts the owner to conclude that these workers would want him to lose his vineyard or his harvest, and certainly the income from them! These first-hired workers are behaving shamefully with their complaint. They did, after all, receive exactly what they had bargained for.

Other related examples of the evil eye manifesting envy and resentment of the good fortune of others are:

Proverbs 23:6–8

Wisdom 4:12

Sirach 14:3, 5–7, 8, 9

Sirach 31:13

Sirach 37:11

Genesis 37:11

Other New Testament occurrences of the evil-eye phrase are:

Matthew 6:22–23

Luke 11:33–34

Mark 7:22

On the basis of what you have learned about the evil eye try to explain the significance of evil eye in each of these contexts.

The vineyard owner asks whether the first-hired are envious or jealous (have an evil eye), because he is "generous." Some scholars point out that a denarius is hardly generous even if given to the last-hired who worked the least time. This interpretation, however, is rooted in a western idea of value that is calculated quantitatively. "Generosity" as a Mediterranean value does not have to do with quantity so much as with the nature and quality of a special relationship known as "patronage."

C. Patronage, the Patron-Client Relationship, or Economics Rooted in Kinship

A corollary of the notion of "limited good" is the belief that anyone who is lucky enough to realize a sudden fortune is expected to immediately distribute this "increase" in goods so that his possessions will remain always the same. Thus, in Luke 12:15–21, Jesus cautions against the stinginess of a man who built barns to hoard his bumper crop, thereby increasing his good at the expense of others, instead of distributing the surplus to others as the culture required and expected.

In fact, this stingy man in Luke is the exact opposite of the generous vineyard owner in Matthew. Generous? Yes, generous to the last-hired as he was fair to the first-hired (see Matthew 20:13). Take careful note of the contrasting values: fairness and generosity. Generosity is a characteristic of a "patron" but not of an "employer."

In the peasant society of Palestine at the time of Jesus, extremely wealthy landowners provided the landless with land and/or work in exchange for a specific return: either a portion of the harvest or a wage. In practice, this employer-employee arrangement frequently fell short of human needs, even though it was fair. Still, the landowner owed nothing more to the landless than what was agreed upon, and the landless worker was not obliged to show respect, affection or friendly feelings to the landowner.

Yet what counts more than anything in this society is respect or honor. The landowner looks for such respect or honor, but clearly it will not come from a contract.

Instead, honor and respect come from "favoritism." The landowner chooses to be "generous" to certain workers, to show them "favoritism," and thus enters into a relationship of patron and client with them. As patron, the landowner will see to it that the clients never want for anything. In return, the clients will sing the praises of their patron throughout all the land, thus establishing, maintaining and augmenting the honor of their patron.

In this story of the vineyard workers, the vineyard owner clearly has chosen to become patron to the last-hired group. The discovery of this fact by the first-hired group is a shock. Faithful and devoted contract workers that they are, they deceived themselves into thinking they were more than contract workers. The crunch of this parable is that these contract workers were nothing more than that. And the vineyard owner, like all wealthy landowners in that place and culture, is free to become patron to whomever he chooses.

To sum up, we may say that natives of Mediterranean culture—whether those addressed immediately by Jesus, or the crowds who listened to the apostolic preachers, or the communities for whom the evangelists produced their version of the gospel—all would include the following elements in the scenario which they would bring to the story of the vineyard workers. Indeed, Jesus, the preachers and the evangelists could count on the fact that these elements would be known, understood and supplied to the story with such certitude that there was no need to mention any of them specifically in the story. The one who has ears to hear, will hear the following:

1. Honor and shame, the core values of Mediterranean culture, which govern this story from beginning to end.

2. Limited good, the belief that all goods are finite in number and already distributed. It is shameful to try to increase one's goods at the expense of others, but quite honorable to attempt to gain what one needs from those in a position to bestow it (patrons).

3. The evil eye, a conviction that certain people can cause injury or loss with their physical eye or glance because they would like to deprive other people of the goods which they possess. These people can use the power unintentionally as well as intentionally. This latter category describes malevolent people who focus their evil eye on virtue, possessions, beauty, wisdom, or anything belonging to another person which they personally do not have and don't want the other person to have either.

4. Patron-client relationship or "favoritism" as an honorable way to gain the goods one needs/wants by promot-

ing the honor of the one who is in a position to fulfill these needs/wants. In a patron-client relationship, the patron treats the client "as if" the client were a family member rather than like a stranger!

Church's Guidelines

"The interpreter must investigate what meaning the sacred writer intended to express and actually expressed in particular circumstances as he used contemporary literary forms in accordance with his own time and culture." (Vatican II Document on Revelation, n. 12)

What literary forms and devices have we noted in Matthew 20:1–16?

What elements of his "time and culture" relative to vineyard owners and workers did Matthew intend to express and actually express in this parable?

"For the correct understanding of what the sacred author wanted to assert, due attention must be paid to the customary and characteristic styles of perceiving, speaking, and narrating which prevailed at the time of the sacred writer, and to the customs men normally followed at that period in their everyday dealings with one another." (Vatican II Document on Revelation, n. 12).

What characteristic styles of perceiving have you observed in Matthew 20:1–16?

– the evil-eye?

– generosity?

– fairness?

What customs that people normally followed in their everyday dealings with one another have you learned to see in Matthew 20:1–16?

– vineyard ownership?

– hiring workers?

– looking for a job?

– favoritism?

– fairness?

V. An Interpretation of the Vineyard Workers Parable in the Light of All the Preceding Reflections

The vineyard workers parable can be interpreted at three levels or stages of tradition.

A. Jesus and His Parable

Matthew 20:1–15, which scholars agree is quite likely the parable Jesus told, is yet another instance in the gospels where Jesus characterizes God. "The reign of God," or "the kingdom of heaven" is another way of saying: "This is what God is like."

All human statements about God, however, are based on human experience. Traditional Catholic theology phrases it thus: "All theology is analogy." Everything human beings say about God is rooted in human experience. And human experience is culturally conditioned. So it should come as no surprise that Jesus' statements about God will be colored by his native, Mediterranean culture.

In the vineyard workers parable, the image Jesus uses is drawn from the cultural institution known as patronage: the relationship of a patron and a client. Thus the phrase "the kingdom of heaven" can be interpreted, "This is how God the patron deals with clients," or "The way God's patronage relates and affects his clients is like the following scenario."

Clearly Jesus presents God the patron as being *generous,* just like the vineyard owner is when he acts as patron toward his clients.

This parable in Matthew's story line is actually a good sequel to what preceded, namely, that the wealthy ought never forget to play the role of patron whenever they can. It is no sin to be rich; it is rather a sin to be greedy. The person with great possessions who was unwilling to share them with the poor was in reality greedy rather than generous (Matthew 19:16–30). It is in contrast to this greedy human being that Jesus portrays God as a generous patron and proposed this model for imitation.

Those workers who cast an "evil eye" in this scenario express an unwillingness to accept and still less emulate the divinely presented and sanctioned patterns of benevolence and largess.

In Matthew's story line, God's way of doing things totally inverts and exceeds human ways of doing things ("the first will be last, the last, first" 19:30; 20:16).

Jesus can easily have directed such a story and remarks against the Pharisees, who are the most frequent targets of his criticism in Matthew. Some Pharisees created the impression that God prefers to treat his people like contract workers rather than as clients of a generous patron.

B. The Apostolic Preachers and Jesus' Parable

We already noted the verse which manuscript evidence indicates does not properly belong here: "Many are called, but few are chosen."

This verse may well have been spoken by Jesus. It has a memorable quality, and makes an impressive conclusion. But it seems that no one remembered the original story of which it was the conclusion. Still, it was a good verse to use.

Yet in the light of the invisible elements of Mediterranean culture that fill out this parable's scenario, this verse could be an appropriate ending. While all workers in the vineyard were indeed called or invited to work, as the culture required, some were "chosen" or singled out by the owner for a special relationship, that of client to whom he would be patron.

As Jewish and Gentile converts to Christianity were repeatedly challenged for accepting Jesus as messiah, and Gentile converts in particular were ridiculed as "Johnny-come-lately's" to God's plan, apostolic preachers could do no more than repeat the cultural truism about patrons: they are free to select whom they want as clients.

And as an additional argument, such preachers could also plausibly resort to the baffling reversal pattern that the God of the Bible seemed to enjoy using, e.g., the second born is preferred to the first born, the least become the greatest, the "last will be first, and the first last."

Thus both of these verses form culturally plausible endings to the parable which a preacher could use to skew the story toward a fresh interpretation.

C. Matthew's Use of Jesus' Parable

There is no doubt that the "chiasm" formed by the verses in Matthew 19:30 and 20:16 reveals something about the author's intention. The author deliberately situated this parable in this place in his gospel. What point did he wish to make?

Contemporary scholars generally agree that Matthew was writing between A.D. 80 and 90 primarily for Jewish Christians living in southern Syria. These believers may have very recently been placed outside Judaism by the rabbis of Jamnia (around 80). Such an action would have been a very unsettling experience, a real threat to the victim's faith. Add to this the fact that this new group of believers was also attracting and accepting Gentiles.

In this context, the "first-last" addendum helps this struggling early Christian community to regain a firmer footing and to strengthen their faith in Jesus. It is not at all inconceivable that God could act as the familiar patron of their culture and could elevate the last arrived to a position of prominence.

Thus, to bolster his community's spirits, Matthew has reshaped Jesus' vineyard workers parable with his own ending ("last will be first") and then situated it in his gospel in such a way as to demonstrate that discipleship is given by God and not earned by the candidate. Moreover, the mission to the Gentiles, the "last-hired" of the story, is something willed by God the heavenly patron. Who can quarrel with that?

Conclusion

Following the church's guidelines for interpretation has revealed a wealth of information in the vineyard workers parable which is not immediately evident to western eyes. The church's guidelines are quite general, and their proper application requires much supplementary reading and study. This Bible-study program focuses on the cultural elements, especially insofar as this information enhances the conclusions that can be reached with the traditional historical-critical methods. Readers will agree that the challenge and difficulties of learning new methods and new information can be more than amply rewarded by the stimulating new insights that emerge as a result.

FOLLOW-UP

Reflect on the following:

1. Recall the story of the Jefferson Memorial inscription.

How is biblical interpretation similar or dissimilar to that event?

2. In their Pastoral Statement for Catholics on Biblical Fundamentalism, the United States Bishops caution readers against trying "to find in the Bible all the direct answers for living."

What would this caution mean for an American preacher preparing a homily on this passage for Labor Day?

What would this caution mean for an American worker recently unemployed after many devoted years of faithful service who searches this parable for a message from God?

3. Why is "favoritism" or "nepotism" the normal rule of business in the Middle East but frowned upon and subject to lawsuits in the United States?

4. What steps would you take to help other believers become acquainted with the church's guidelines for interpreting scripture reviewed in this lesson? Remember that scripture and the church's guidelines are intended for all believers and not just for scholars or specialists.

5. Americans are known to be practical, pragmatic, down-to-earth, and concerned about relevance. A recent suggestion for improving the teaching of mathematics in the United States was to make it more relevant to daily life. Above all else, believers want homilies and Bible study to be relevant.

In the search for relevance, how would you interpret this exhortation from the Pontifical Biblical Commission: "When they narrate biblical events let [biblical interpreters] not add imaginative details, which are not consonant with the truth."

How do you think "truth" should be interpreted in this guideline?

Resources

Elliott, John H. "Patronage and Clientism in Early Christian Society: A Short Reading Guide," *Forum* 3 (4, Dec. 1987), 39–48.
Elliott, John H. "The Fear of the Leer: The Evil Eye from the Bible to Li'l Abner," *Forum* 4 (4, Dec. 1988), 42–71.

Ferraro, Gary P. *The Cultural Dimension of International Business*. Englewood Cliffs, N.J.: Prentice-Hall, 1990. This book is especially apt for this session in particular and this Bible-study program in general. The author employs the same cultural concepts that contemporary biblical scholars use in studying Mediterranean culture.

Funk, Robert W. et al. *The Parables of Jesus: Red Letter Edition*. Sonoma, CA.: Polebridge Press, 1988.

Malina, Bruce J. "Patron and Client: The Analogy Behind Synoptic Theology," *Forum* 4 (1, March, 1988), 2–32.

Murdock, George P. *Theories of Illness: A World Survey*. Pittsburgh: University of Pittsburgh Press, 1980.

Oakman, Douglas E. *Jesus and the Economic Questions of His Day*. Studies in the Bible and Early Christianity, 8. Lewiston/Queenston: The Edwin Mellen Press, 1986.

Pilch, John J. "Interpreting Scripture: The Social Science Method," *The Bible Today* (January, 1988), 13–19.

Scott, Bernard Brandon. *Hear Then the Parable: A Commentary on the Parables of Jesus*. Minneapolis: Fortress, 1988.

Session Three

*Overview of the New Testament:
A Mediterranean Cultural Perspective*

From time to time, *The New York Times* prints an instructional block in the newspaper advising readers "How to read *The New York Times*" as follows:

Before reading further, how would you answer this question:

What order do you follow in reading the newspaper?

The New York Times explains:

1. The day's *most important news,* as judged by the editors, is located on the right hand column (*column 6*) on page one. Usually this column runs right under the weather report in the masthead. If this happens to be an international story, then other international news will be grouped near it.

2. The day's *second most important* story appears in the far left-hand column (*column 1*) on page one. If this happens to be a local story, then other local news will be at the left also.

3. The day's *most important national news* story generally appears on the *bottom* of page one, *near the middle.* Other national news also generally appears nearby.

The New York Times then concludes this instruction with this notice: "Not only do you get 'All the News That's Fit to Print,' you get it organized for easy reading."

Wouldn't it be helpful if the New Testament had been "organized for easy reading"? Unfortunately it isn't. In this session, we will learn how the twenty-seven books of the New Testament are organized. At the same time, we will consider some Mediterranean cultural perspectives that can make reading and understanding these clusters of books a little easier.

Preparation: Overview of New Testament organization

Lesson: Cultural perspectives on New Testament books

Follow-up: Read one book from this fresh perspective

PREPARATION

Examine your New Testament. Make a list of the books contained in it, and try to determine how it has been organized.

Is any general division of material apparent?

Does it appear that the gospels are gathered together in a collection, and all non-gospels follow in a second collection?

Modern scholars point out that those who compiled the New Testament as a single book toward the end of the second century made two general divisions: the gospels; and the apostolic writings.

The Gospels

Early manuscripts of the New Testament used in the western church reveal that the gospel sequence was: Matthew, John, Luke and Mark. The first two gospels were attributed to apostles, the last two gospels were attributed to disciples of the apostles.

In the current order of gospels, Matthew, Mark and Luke are placed together because they are synoptic gospels. This means that their roughly similar composition makes it easy to compare them when they are placed side by side, or when one reads them one after another. A careful reader begins to identify parallel passages in these gospels. John is not so easily compared with these three, and thus is presented last in the order of gospels.

From your knowledge or study of the gospels, do you know or have you learned that modern scholars consider Luke's gospel and Acts of the Apostles as a single composition, understood properly only when read in sequence as a single composition?

With this understanding of Luke-Acts in mind, does the insertion of John's gospel between Luke and Acts of the Apostles "organize" this section of the New Testament "for easy reading"?

Paul's Letters

Examine the collection of letters in your New Testament beginning with Romans and ending with Hebrews.

How many letters are there?

Leaving Hebrews aside for a moment, how do the rest of Paul's letters seem to be organized or arranged?

Does it seem that Paul's letters to churches are presented first (Romans to Thessalonians), and then Paul's letters to individuals (Timothy, Titus, Philemon)?

Does the relative length of the letters in each collection seem to play a role in how they are organized?

Do you think that the letters are arranged from the longest to the shortest in each category (churches; individuals)?

In what sense could this arrangement serve "for easy reading"?

In what sense does such an arrangement of the letters contribute to more difficult reading, understanding, and interpretation?

Remaining New Testament Writings by other "Apostles": James, 1–2; Peter, 1–2–3; John; Jude; Revelation

The General Letters to the Churches

In very early manuscripts of the New Testament, the seven letters which bear the names of James, Peter, John and Jude always appeared clustered together. They, too, seem to have been ordered roughly according to length from longest to shortest.

Revelation

Finally, in these same early manuscripts, the Apocalypse, or book of Revelation, often stood apart. Though it has features of a letter, and includes letters to seven churches, it is in reality what its opening words claim: a revelation. Those familiar with this book of the New Testament will admit that no matter where it is placed in any order of books, understanding and interpreting this book still poses a challenge.

Summarizing Conclusion

Unlike *The New York Times*, the books of the New Testament do not strike the modern reader as having been organized "for easy reading." Anyone who has ever resolved to read the New Testament in sequence has experienced the difficulty in remembering what was read where (e.g., "Is this verse in a gospel or an epistle?" "Which one?") and keeping it all straight (e.g., "How does Matthew's report of Jesus' temptation differ from that of Luke? How do both differ from Mark?")

Even those familiar with the Bible, such as bishops, priests and teachers, often misidentify passages. In his regular newspaper column, one bishop assigned to Paul a passage found only in the gospels. In a prayer service designed by religious educators, there is a reference to something Paul taught us in Acts of the Apostles! (Though he figures prominently in Acts of the Apostles, Paul did not write the book, nor is he the one who speaks the sentence attributed to him in the prayer service.) The sentence is not a quote from Paul. It is simply part of Luke's narrative.

Those who attempt to rearrange the New Testament in an approximate chronological order of composition so that readers might better appreciate the circumstances in which our scriptures arose only introduce new difficulties, along with any imagined benefit of this new arrangement.

First, the calendar according to which this new arrangement is made simply did not exist at the time the New Testament was being lived and written. In other words, the modern American custom of reckoning time by decades (the 1950s, the 1960s, the 1970s etc.) and characterizing each decade (for instance, the '70s = the "ME" decade) is inappropriately applied to the New Testament period.

For example, consider the destruction of the Jerusalem Temple in A.D. 70 (on our calendar) which culminated the First Jewish War extending between 66 and 70. Did this event end the "60s" or begin the "70s"?

Might there be a better way of identifying New Testament events? In *Hear the Word*! Book One, Session Seven, I pointed out that Old Testament "history" was reported in "relationship patterns." When so and so was king here, this happened. Much of the New Testament is similarly reported. "When I come to you ... " or, "At that time a dispute arose among the silversmiths ... "

Second, each book of the New Testament has a "history" of its own. The gospels, for instance, include oral traditions that reach back to Jesus as well as to the early preachers. The evangelists also utilized already written sources in their own compositions, and these written sources also give evidence of development. To assign Matthew's gospel the date "A.D. 80" not only places it on an inappropriate calendar but also blurs the decades-long development of the traditions captured in Matthew's composition.

While it isn't fair to follow *The New York Times* suggestion that a proper "order" of the New Testament books could contribute to an "easier reading," some familiarity with Mediterranean culture can make the New Testament easier to read and understand and even more enjoyable.

For instance:

READ the three synoptic versions of the story of Jesus' healing of the paralytic and compare the following verses which tell how the petitioner is brought into Jesus' presence:

Matthew 9:1–2

Where is Jesus?

How is the paralytic brought to him?

Mark 2:4

Where is Jesus?

How is the paralytic brought to him?

Luke 5:19

Where is Jesus?

How is the paralytic brought to him?

Here are three versions of one event in Jesus' life. The verse in question relates to a minor detail of the story, but a detail which was considered important enough to have to be "culturally" correct lest the entire story lose credibility.

Did you notice that Mark had people digging a hole in the roof, while Luke said the people removed tiles?

Mark's description reflects the common Palestinian house, made of wooden beams which were placed across stone or mudbrick walls. These beams were then covered with reeds, layers of thorns, and several inches of clay. The roof had a slight slope, and was usually rolled before the rainy season (late September to early May).

Did you notice that Luke mentioned "tiles" on the roof?

Scholars agree that Luke changed Mark's description in order to reflect the custom of having tiled roofs on Hellenistic houses in the eastern Mediterranean world. Greek-speaking Christians who were unfamiliar with Palestinian mud roofs would find Mark's version of the story amusing and even "unreal." Luke's mention of a tile roof reflects the urban custom familiar to these Greek-speaking Christians who would have been distracted by the mud roof and would not have paid attention to the real point of the story.

These two verses provide a small peek into some cultural differences between our world and the Mediterranean world of our biblical ancestors in the faith. They also illustrate differences in different regions of that rather large world. Information of this nature is easily found in standard commentaries and Bible encyclopedias. In this present session, we will consider some common Mediterranean cultural strategies that will enhance the reading of the New Testament books, no matter what order a reader chooses.

LESSON

A. Name-Calling in Matthew's Gospel: An Exercise in Honor and Shame

The core values of the Mediterranean world are honor and shame. Honor is a public claim to worth accompanied by public affirmation of that claim. If the public denies the claim to honor, that person is publicly shamed.

Mediterranean people regularly engage in an activity of publicly challenging others in the hope that the one challenged might be unable to respond and will therefore be publicly shamed. Such a successful challenger gains prestige or honor from the crowd which recognizes the challenger's superior position. Thus this strategy of "challenge and response" is one means of attacking the honor of another in the hopes of enhancing one's own honor. It also included the risk of failure and therefore being shamed.

Calling other people names, whether honorable, like "Son of David!" (Matthew 21:9) or shameful, like "glutton and drunkard" (Matthew 11:19) is a challenge to their honor. The one challenged must make an appropriate response. When the name is honorable, the honored one must demonstrate proper humility ("Only God alone is good!" Read Mark 10:17–31) and allow others, like bystanders, to affirm the compliment. When the name is shameful, an insult, the one insulted must make a witty comeback to save face or else the public affirmation of shame will stick! Consider the following passages.

READ these verses and note who calls Jesus by what name:

Matthew 9:3

How does Jesus parry the challenge?

Matthew 9:34

If there is no response, who wins this challenge?

Matthew 10:24–25

Do these verses hearken back to 9:34?

Matthew 11:18–19

Is there a response to the challenge here?

Matthew 12:22–37, esp. verse 24:

Does Jesus' response parry the challenge successfully?

Matthew 12:38–45

A "question" is always perceived to be a challenge in the Mediterranean world. Questions are rarely neutral requests for information.

Does Jesus parry the challenge successfully?

Read and compare Matthew 23:1–39 with all the verses just read.

List all the challenges (insults) hurled by Jesus against the scribes and Pharisees.

Does anyone make a response?

Reading Matthew's gospel with an eye to "challenges and responses" makes it clear that Jesus can give as good as he gets. He always manages to ward off the challenge. Up until Matthew 26, the passion story, Jesus' chief opponents are the scribes and Pharisees. The game of "challenge and response" between Jesus and his opponents seems to end in a draw. They never managed to discredit Jesus, and Jesus never managed to blow them totally away.

In the passion story, a new set of opponents emerges: "the chief priests and the elders of the people" (Matthew 26:3–5). These opponents successfully pin two labels on Jesus: "blasphemer" (Matthew 26:65) and "throne-pretender" (Matthew 27:11–14) which ultimately results in his execution by a most shameful death.

That Jesus was raised from death by God restores Jesus' honor in an indisputable way. And the gospel of Matthew, written with hindsight many years after Jesus' death and resurrection, retroactively reinterprets Jesus' trial as an occasion for revealing Jesus' true, honorable, God-pleasing identity: "Truly this was the Son of God!" (Matthew 27:54).

Conclusion

Focusing on the core Mediterranean values of honor and shame, and paying special attention to the strategy of challenge and response in the quest for honor offers a fresh perspective on the gospel of Matthew. One can also read Paul's letters and other parts of the New Testament from a similar perspective and anticipate similar results as gained in Matthew.

B. Paul is "all things to all people" (1 Corinthians 9:22): A typical, Mediterranean, group-oriented (other-directed) personality

The strong sense of individualism that characterizes American culture is almost totally lacking in the Mediterranean world. There human beings perceive themselves primarily in terms of the *groups* to which they belong: family, disciples, etc. They are primarily group-oriented or group-centered. Individual desires, wishes, aspirations, hopes, plans, all are subject to group consideration and approval or rejection. In our western culture, we would call such people "other-directed," or incapable of standing on their own two feet.

Scholars call such group-oriented individuals "dyadic personalities." The word "dyad" means pair. A dyadic personality always needs another person or persons to assure personal identity, to grant social approval, to assist in making decisions, to prevent one from getting into trouble, to monitor behavior, etc.

Paul the apostle is such a dyadic personality. The people (churches and individuals) to whom he has addressed his letters are also dyadic personalities. Here are a few select passages from Paul's letters to help you learn more about such persons.

READ 1 Thessalonians:

1:6

How many people are writing this letter (see verse 1)?

How do these letter-writers perceive themselves (see verse 6) in relationship to the letter-receivers?

What role do they expect the letter-receivers to play?

How does this compare to the American emphasis on "being my own person"; "I am master of my destiny"; etc.?

5:14

To whom is this verse addressed?

How would one judge when another person is "idle," "fainthearted," or "weak"?

Would the "fainthearted," "idle," and "weak" admit these deficiencies and accept these labels?

Did you ever read or hear that any of Paul's letter-receivers complained about or rejected this kind of exhortation?

Does the advice here seem like everybody should mind everybody else's business?

How would you as an American respond to this kind of person in your parish community? Would it matter if that person is pastor, school principal, director of religious education, pastoral minister, Holy Name Society member, or usher?

READ Galatians:

1:10

What does Paul say about his relationships to other human beings?

Whom is Paul trying to please?

2:6

What does this verse say about the way in which a person achieves standing or respect in the community?

Does the passive voice offer a clue?

2:9

If Paul is not trying to please human beings, or is not concerned with what others think, why does he bother to present the information in this verse and its context (2:1–10)?

Might it be because other-directed individuals like Paul always need another person to give assurance to one's determination?

Is it possible at all in this honor-and-shame based society to do one's own thing, go off on one's own, totally ignore public opinion?

4:10

How do other-directed or group-oriented people make a decision?

Do the individuals in this verse stand alone or represent groups?

Is Paul appealing to an individual or to a group?

6:1

Notice again the assumption behind this verse that it is fair game to "mind other people's business."

READ 1 Corinthians:

1:11–17; 3:3–4

What groups in Corinth have the group-oriented personalities joined?

Why is Paul stressed when they are "behaving like ordinary human beings" (3:3) in this matter?

Is there a clue for the answer in verse 7?

Does belonging to a group give a person some status, prestige or standing (note the phrase "to be anything")?

Recall that honor and shame are group possessions, group characterizations. Individuals who belong to the group share in the group's honor and are capable of shaming the group as well. Hence, it is only "normal" (Paul calls this "ordinary") for a group to seek to highlight its claim to honor, to fame.

To whom does Paul prefer that the honor be given?

3:16–17

Note well that the Greek verbs in this verse are plural, hence a literal translation would be: Do you (plural) not know that you (plural) are (plural form of the verb) God's temple, and the spirit of God dwells within you (plural)? If any one destroys God's temple (= the community, recall the plural just above), God will destroy that one. God's temple (= community) is holy, and you (plural) are (plural form of the verb) that temple.

In the light of what you have learned about the Mediterranean "group-oriented" or "group-centered" personality, how would you interpret this well-known passage?

Who, then, is the temple of God?

Where does God's spirit abide?

How does a group-centered person fit into this scheme?

Compare these verses with 6:12–20, especially verse 19.

What kind of behavior is Paul trying to discourage?

Would this behavior harm an individual or harm a community?

Does Paul mention here the risk of sexually-transmitted diseases?

What does Paul mention?

Does Paul raise a personal consequence or the consequence for the group, the Christian community?

How do you think a group-centered or group-oriented individual would react to someone who points out the damage an action works on the group?

Are you surprised to learn that a group-oriented person would actually be motivated to behave properly out of regard for the group's welfare, rather than for personal rewards?

5:1–5

Notice again that while one person is singled out, the plural verbs in verse 2 indicate the group is proud of this member's conduct.

Is it fair to say that the dyadic personality singled out in Paul's criticism is destroying God's temple, that is, God's community, by his behavior?

9:19–23

Read this passage over very carefully. It well describes the typical, Mediterranean, dyadic personality: one who is always subject to the needs of the group.

Notice how the entire passage is summed up in the concluding sentence of verse 22.

Do you have any relatives, friends or acquaintances who adopt this approach to life?

Would this be the key to success in America?

10:23—11:1

Notice verse 24: here is the glowing example of a group-oriented, Mediterranean person.

How does this compare with the American way of life?

Notice also verse 29: another illustration of a Mediterranean, dyadic personality.

Whose conscience do you follow?

Conclusion

Paul is very definitely a man of his culture. He is interested in maintaining his honor and avoiding shame. One characteristic of the honorable Mediterranean person is deference to the needs of the group. Usually, the word "group" means the immediate group: family, faction, village, neighborhood of a city, and not necessarily the total ethnic group.

In this section, verses from some of Paul's letters were taken out of the complete letter. If time allows, the reader is encouraged to read the letters in their entirety in order to become familiar with Thessalonika, Corinth and Galatia, and the groups with which Paul had to cope during his missionary work. These are the same groups his converts had to cope with in Paul's absence. It is this larger context that forms the broader honor-and-shame framework of each letter.

Notice that behavior controls in Paul's Mediterranean world are *external* (public opinion) and not *internal* (a sense of guilt) as they are with us. Other people apply external pressures to guarantee desired behaviors. This involves such things as physically removing a sinner from the community, as in 1 Corinthians 5. Everyone minding everyone else's business is surely a very strong social pressure for behavior in this society.

How is American society different?

How, then, can Americans be good, Bible-inspired Christians?

This group-oriented dimension of personality is visible in the gospels and in other parts of the New Testament as well. As time allows, select additional passages in the New Testament in which you might meet other group-oriented personalities like Paul.

C. Maintaining Honor in a Very Public and "Nosey" Community: The Strategy of Secrecy and Deception

It is only in a wide-open society like that of the circum-Mediterranean world where most of life is lived outdoors in public view that honor and shame could exist as core values. Honor and shame are publicly proclaimed, reviewed and judged. In such a society, everybody makes it a point to know everything about everybody else. Recall how frequently Paul reminded those who received his letters to keep an eye on others so that they behave properly. And he also reminded them to behave properly themselves so that others would be suitably impressed.

There are two kinds of honor:

1. *ascribed*, or that which derives from birth or deputation; and

2. *achieved*, or that which derives from initiative or achievement.

Ascribed honor is relatively enduring; it is often displayed by means of one's genealogy. Achieved honor is more precarious. The name-calling game in which Jesus and his opponents engaged resulted in achieved (or diminished) honor.

But if society does not recognize privacy, and everybody knows—and continually monitors!—everything about everybody else, what's the sense of making a public claim to worth? Wouldn't that worth or honor be rather obvious and well known to all?

One way of achieving some measure of privacy in such a wide-open society is by the use of deception. Remember that honor is a group quality; individuals participate in the honor of the group. Hence the group, for instance the family, and its members strive mightily to deceive others about information that could damage the group's honor. This deception sometimes takes the form of a lie which is defined as a "technique for restricting the public dissemination of information over a period of time."

Here are illustrations of eight kinds of deception used by Mediterranean people as a legitimate strategy in the service of maintaining or gaining honor.

1. Concealment of failure. Certain deceptions are intended to conceal the failure of an individual or group to live up to the highest ideals or requirements of the social code.

READ Matthew 21:28–32.

Which of these two sons gave an honorable or respectful response?

Which son gave a shameful or disrespectful response?

The point of honor in this story lies in the encounter of the father with both his sons. The son who said "I go" but did not go lied so that he might maintain the honorable, public appearance of an "obedient" son. In honor and shame, appearances count even more than reality. Though in reality this second son was disobedient, in appearance he was obedient and therefore honorable.

Pay careful attention to Jesus' question in verse 31, and the disciples' correct answer. Is Jesus asking about honor, or something else?

Do you think Jesus deliberately bypassed the "honor" consideration to get at another important consideration?

True obedience, as in the case of the first son, can be honorable behavior. But in this story one or two things are lacking. The first son did not make a claim to honor. "I will not go," he said. Second, if he were working all alone in the vineyard there would have been no public to see his honorable behavior and award him with a grant of honor. All that was publicly shown was the expression of disobedience to his father.

2. Concealment of unintentional failure. What does one do *after* one has put one's foot in one's mouth? How does one save face after an unintended flop?

READ Luke 10:25–29.

In the Mediterranean world, a question is routinely interpreted as a challenge.

Who asks the question of Jesus?

What is the questioner's special area of knowledge?

Jesus responds to this challenge with an insulting counter-question. What is this question?

What is the lawyer's response?

READ Leviticus 19:18 very carefully.

In Leviticus 19:18, which the lawyer is quoting in Luke 10:27, who is the neighbor? The two parts of this verse are parallel to each other. Who is parallel to "neighbor"?

By accepting and applauding the lawyer's answer, Jesus has publicly caused the lawyer's strategy for shaming Jesus to fail. It was, of course, an unintended failure.

Consider carefully the lawyer's follow-up question in verse 29. Has he not already indicated that he knows the answer to this question?

Is his second question, then, a deception or a lie, striving now to conceal his very apparent unintentional failure?

3. False imputation. In the United States, it is often said that the best defense is an offense. Certain lies or deceptions guard or maintain honor by denigrating or shaming a competitor.

READ John 8:31–49.

Opinion about Jesus in divided. See John 7:10–13.

Note the Judean claim to honor in John 8:39. Recall that ascribed honor derives from birth.

What is Jesus' response in John 8:39–40?

What is the next Judean claim to honor in John 8:41?

What is Jesus' insulting response in John 8:44?

Is this a serious challenge to honor? How serious is a challenge to another person's birth-origins?

What is the lie and deception the Judeans resort to in order to preserve their honor which Jesus has attacked? READ John 8:48.

Honor is of such great importance in Mediterranean culture that deception and lying are legitimate strategies used in defense of honor. If one loses honor, one might as well be dead. Here the Judeans voice a lie of false imputation about Jesus' origins in an effort to protect their own honor.

4. Avoiding quarrels or trouble. In honor-and-shame cultures, quarrels are always capable of escalating to violence which could result in someone's death. Since no one really ever wants a quarrel to reach this point, some deceptions and lies are pressed into service to avoid a quarrel or escape trouble.

READ Matthew 26:69–75.

Matthew's version of Peter's threefold denial of Jesus reveals additional dimensions of the common use of deception or lies. In this instance, Peter clearly wants to stay out of trouble.

Notice the very public dimension of this scene. There are bystanders in whose presence the three accusations or challenges are made. Honor and shame are inextricably present in this scene.

What is Peter's first response "before all" in verse 70?

What is Peter's second response "to the bystanders" in verse 71?

What in this response is different from the first response?

Because deception and lying are such common strategies for maintaining and safeguarding honor, the core Mediterranean cultural value, the real challenge in this culture is to know when someone is telling the truth!

RECALL Matthew 5:33–37. Jesus proposes simple truthfulness as the hallmark of his disciples.

RECALL Leviticus 19:12. God does not want to be called as a witness to a lie or a deception.

Would the bystanders be swayed by Peter's oath?

What is Peter's third response to the "bystanders" in verse 74?

Pronouncing a curse upon oneself is one of the strategies used by a speaker to confirm that truth is being told.

READ Ruth 1:15–18.

How does Naomi confirm that she truly wants to remain with Ruth, does not want to leave her? See especially verse 17 where Naomi invokes a curse on herself to validate her promise as genuine and firm.

Peter is, of course, lying through his teeth in this episode. He utilizes the legitimate strategy of deception and lie to avoid trouble and therefore safeguard his honor. After all, Peter publicly boasted to Jesus: "I will never fall away," and "Even if I must die with you, I will not deny you" as did all the disciples (Matthew 26:30–35).

With regard to the maids and bystanders in Peter's denial scene, the purpose of his lie is *avoid trouble*. To admit he is a disciple might bring him to the same difficulty Jesus is facing. It is also possible that others among the bystanders may have been aware of Peter and the other disciples making public pledges of fidelity to Jesus which Peter has clearly broken. For such listeners (and the evangelist's original, Mediterranean listeners/readers), Peter's lie takes on an additional function. Peter tries to cover up his unintentional failure to fulfill his boast (Matthew 26:30–35) and to stay with Jesus after the arrest in the garden (26:47–56). Deception in Mediterranean culture is a spontaneous and unreflective strategy that springs forward to defend honor whenever it is threatened.

5. For gain. Honor is also reckoned in part by material possessions. This would be achieved honor, gained by cheating on a deal or by pretending to be cunning and shrewd.

READ 1 Kings 21.

Why does Naboth refuse to accept the king's offer regarding his vineyard? (See verse 3.)

What role does Naboth's vineyard play in his honor rating?

What happens to the king's honor rating when his subject refuses a king's offer?

How does the king respond to the refusal? Is he shamed?

How does Jezebel, the king's wife, respond to the refusal? (See verses 8–14.)

What kind of lie is that of Jezebel?

What kind of lie is that of the two false witnesses?

In terms of honor, how has King Ahab's reputation as a ruler been preserved?

Jezebel was truly cunning and shrewd. With her lies, she was able to do away with the man who shamed the king by refusing his offers. The king's honorable reputation as an effective ruler is preserved by the death-dealing deception of Jezebel. The king is able to increase his possessions and thereby also augment his honor.

6. Sheer concealment. The ruthless community curiosity stimulated by this pervasive strategy of deception in the service of honor generates yet another type of deception prompted by the unknown power of the nosey community. In time this strategy is honed and practiced just for the fun of it.

READ John 7:1–10.

In the busy-body of Mediterranean culture, if the community knows your plans in advance, they may take action to thwart you or aggravate you. For this reason, plans and intentions of any kind are kept secret.

Notice the "honor" motivation which Jesus' brothers suggest so that he should travel from Galilee to Jerusalem for the feast of Tabernacles. (See verses 3–4.)

What is Jesus' response in verses 8–9?

What does Jesus eventually do in verse 10?

Did Jesus simply change his mind? Or is it probable that Jesus has engaged in a deception about his plans to keep his enemies off balance?

News gets around, and if he were to let his plans be known in advance, Jerusalemites would be prepared for him. As it is, the text indicates (verse 11) that the Judeans were indeed expecting him and looking for him at the feast.

7. Pure mischief, or to confuse authorities. For some people in an honor-and-shame society, their claim to honor is an exceptional skill in this basic strategy of deception.

READ 2 Timothy 3:1–17.

Make a list of the deceptions that some people will practice "in the last days." (See verses 2–5, 8, 13.)

What impressions do you draw from this list? Do these deceivers appear to enjoy what they are doing?

How can a believer avoid confusion? (See verses 14–17.)

Even though excellence in deception, a strategy integral to maintaining honor, gives an expert deceiver a claim to honor, the targets of this deception have to work all the harder not to be taken in by it. At stake is nothing less than their own honor! In this society, honor and not money is the greatest form of wealth.

8. On behalf of friend, guest, or kin. Honor being a group-centered quality, it is obvious that deception is certainly a useful strategy in protecting the honor of a group.

READ Joshua 2.

Hospitality in the Middle East is extended primarily to *strangers*. The purpose of hospitality is to grant a stranger safe passage through a region where he is automatically under deep suspicion of being up to no good, simply because he is not kin to anyone and not known by anyone.

Hospitality is ordinarily given by the strong man in the community.

READ Joshua 2:1.

What deceptive purpose might lie behind the spies' decision to lodge with Rahab the harlot instead of with a strong man of the village?

Would this be a good way to throw suspicious city administrators or security guards off guard?

Summarize Rahab's deception as presented in verses 4–7.

Why did Rahab lie about these spies? (See verses 14–17.)

From one perspective, then, Rahab's lie can be viewed as a lie for gain. (See deception number 5 above.)

However, it must be remembered that the process of Middle-Eastern hospitality can have two outcomes: first, the stranger is transformed into temporary guest and may leave as a friend; second, the stranger is transformed into temporary guest and may leave again as stranger. The outcome depends upon the entire experience. Sparse as it is, verse 2 may conceal the events by which Rahab and her guests become friends. This unknown event or events then acted as a second motivation for Rahab to lie on their behalf.

Honor can be achieved by making friends. This achieved honor can then be augmented by defending one's friends even with the customary strategy of deception in its varied forms.

Conclusion

Just as the Mediterranean core values of honor and shame permeate the Bible from beginning to end, so too do deception and lying, key strategies for safeguarding, maintaining, and augmenting honor as needed. The reader is invited to keep the strategy of deception in mind, too, in reading other books of the Bible.

Conclusion to the Lesson

The New Testament is of sufficiently manageable size that a reader can easily learn the distinctive organization of its twenty-seven books. This knowledge helps a reader find what is being sought with relative ease and without the need of looking first at the table of contents.

The reader interested in acquiring new skills in reading and interpreting the books of the New Testament will find that concentrating on honor and shame, the core Mediterranean values, will be of fundamental importance. Learning how the cultural strategies of name-calling and deception are readily used in acquiring and safeguarding honor provides the Bible reader with some very basic tools that facilitate an authentic reading and respectful interpretation of these ancient texts. This, even more than the order of the New Testament's organization, makes for easier reading.

FOLLOW-UP

1. Return again to the New Testament and thumb through its pages to become even more familiar with the "order" in which the books are gathered.

2. With the aid of a commentary, or the notes in your New Testament, make a list of the "Chronological" order in which one might arrange the gospels; Paul's letters; the remaining writings of the New Testament.

3. Unlike *The New York Times*, it may not be helpful to recommend a special "order" of New Testament books which would make for easier reading. But as an alternative, some key insights drawn from cross-cultural studies can facilitate reading and understanding New Testament documents. How many such insights have you learned already?

4. Read through John 7 and 8 and compile a list of "name-calling" strategies that appear therein. Try to assess the impact of the exchanges upon the honor of each party (Jesus; the Judeans).

5. Read Romans 12–15 from a perspective of "group-centered" or "dyadic" personality. How does this perspective contribute to an understanding of "the strong in the faith" and "the weak in the faith"?

6. Read the letters to the churches in Revelation 1–3. Make a list of and seek to categorize the deceptions or lies charged against each congregation.

Resources

Pilch, John J. *Hear the Word!* Book One. New York/Mahwah: Paulist Press, 1991. Session Three on honor and shame; Session Five on "group-centered" personality; Session Seven on a different view of time.

Malina, Bruce J. and Jerome H. Neyrey. *Calling Jesus Names.* Sonoma, CA: Polebridge Press, 1988.

Neyrey, Jerome H., S.J., ed. *The Social World of Luke Acts: Models for Interpretation.* Peabody, MA: Hendrickson Publishers, 1991. Chapter Three: First Century Personality: Dyadic, Not Individualistic.

Session Four

Values and Human Activity

A Case Study

A young sales affiliate in a multinational corporation who volunteered for an overseas assignment was sent to negotiate a deal in Saudi Arabia. Upon his arrival, the host escorted him to a plush and pleasant hotel. The host said the business meeting was scheduled for Thursday, a full two days after his late afternoon arrival on Monday. The host encouraged him to rest and relax until then.

The eager sales affiliate was very disappointed to learn of this arrangement. He insisted that he was prepared to make his presentation immediately on Tuesday morning. He felt sufficiently rested. The host reluctantly agreed to change the arrangements.

On Tuesday morning, the eager sales affiliate got right down to business and pitched his product with all his might. He was troubled that his audience appeared to be impassive and showed only polite interest in him. They had, after all, requested this information.

When his presentation was ended, there was no discussion. The group disbanded.

On Tuesday afternoon he was informed that the Saudi firm had decided against accepting his company's offer.

On the return trip home, the dejected sales associate replayed his experience over and over in his imagination, trying to discern what went wrong.

What is your judgment? What do you think went wrong?

This fictionalized case study based on an actual experience represents one aspect of the education and training which is intended to help students prepare for business careers in today's expanding international market. It is also similar to the kind of education and training intended to help health care professionals learn how to deliver western, scientific health care to clients from varying cultural and ethnic backgrounds such as the Hmong, Thais, or Haitians who now live in the United States.

Contemporary biblical scholars have been designing similar education and training programs to develop a cross-cultural sensitivity that would help readers to respect and appreciate the Bible's distinctive Mediterranean cultural flavor.

To return to the introductory case study, the reason why the energetic American sales affiliate was unsuccessful in Saudi Arabia can be found in a clash of basic values. Americans hold energetic, purposeful activity in high esteem. An American wants to get down to business without wasting time, deal and negotiate with drive and gusto, and nail the deal down as quickly as possible. A single word often used to describe this value is "doing." Americans above all are "doers."

Saudis, like Middle Easterners in general, put a much higher priority on human relationships, on taking time to become acquainted and to establish a friendship, and on leisure. In due time, the business deal will work itself out. But everything in due time. The single word often used to describe this value is "being," that is, a spontaneous and uninhibited response to the challenge of the present moment. Middle Easterners are truly expert at just "being."

The American and his Saudi hosts both came "ready to play," to borrow a phrase from contemporary American sports. But in the American athletic arena, "play" means hard work and business. In the arena of Saudi culture, "play" means play, responding to the stimulus of the present moment. The American failed to respond to his Saudi host's cue. This failure cost the sales associate's firm some highly desirable and profitable business.

In this session, we will focus on *three forms of human activity* and explore different perceptions and assessments of these activities across cultures.

Preparation: The American preference for doing

Lesson: The Mediterranean preference for being

Follow-up: Further contrasts of doing and being

PREPARATION

All cultures take a distinctive orientation toward five basic human challenges:

1. modes of human activity;

2. ways of relating to others;

3. a temporal preference;

4. nature as distinct from human beings;

5. human nature.

Each of these challenges will be reviewed from a cross-cultural perspective in the next chapters. In this chapter we begin with modes of human activity.

The ways human beings can address each of these challenges are not infinite in number. Actually, there are only three choices for each challenge. For instance, with regard to human activity, groups can choose from:

Doing—a basic orientation toward activity, calculated according to a plan with a view to reaching some goal within a very specific time frame.

Being—activity that is characterized by lack of planning and having no long-range goal in view at all. Such human activity is totally spontaneous, responding to the challenge of the moment.

Being in becoming—an orientation toward human activity that seeks to respond to all challenges as they occur. This orientation is interested in developing all human potentials equally. Leonardo da Vinci is known to have begun an engineering project, then switched to a painting, and then without having completed either of these projects, turned his attention to yet another project: anatomical dissection. In this value option, developing different interests and maneuvering successfully through stages of development are more important than getting the job done.

Cultures differ in the way they arrange the choices. This is a key to interpreting the scriptures respectfully. American culture differs from Mediterranean cultures.

Before continuing, it would be helpful to clarify the use of and understanding of some key phrases in *Hear the Word!* I use the phrase "mainstream United States culture" to describe the prevalent value options in the United States. Sometimes I use the phrase "middle-class American culture," and at other times I use the phrase "American culture." The word, "American," generally describes much more than the United States, for it also includes Canada, Mexico, and even Central and South America. When I use the word "American" in this program, it is intended only as a variation on "mainstream United States culture." Clearly the culture of Canada, Mexico, and the countries of Central and South America differ from one another. Readers whose ethnic roots stem from these cultures are encouraged to explore their cultural distinctiveness according to the models that will be explained here and in the remaining chapters. These differences are important and very meaningful. But for present purposes, we seek to generalize about the United States.

The same is true with our use of the word, "Mediterranean culture." Experts such as Raphael Patai and David Gilmore agree that it is quite legitimate to speak of this region in such general terms. For Patai, the Middle East is a *cultural concept*. The geographic region it comprises extends from the Atlantic Ocean on the west; the Mediterranean, the Black Sea, the Caucasus, the Caspian Sea, the Turkish Kazakh, and Tadzhik Soviet Republics on the north; the Indus River on the east; the Arabian Sea on the southeast; and the Sudan belt on the south.

Gilmore summarizes the opinion of leading experts on the Mediterranean world when he notes that the Mediterranean Basin represents a *cultural unity*. It is a true culture area, that is, a bounded entity forged through millennia of contact, exchange, intermarriage and mutual colonizations.

Of course, there are distinctive differences between countries, as well as between groups within countries. These differences, however, are not like the difference between night and day, but are rather differences more like variations on a theme. The theme is always present and identifiable. It is simply played out in different ways.

In preparation for this present session, we focus on the arrangement of choices relative to human activity that characterize mainstream U.S. or middle-class American culture.

DOING	BEING	BEING-IN-BECOMING
work and job are critical	making friends and enjoying life are critical	developing all dimensions of human potential is critical
nose to the grindstone attitude	"sweet idleness" (*dolce far niente*; *mañana*)	begin a new task before completing a previous task
competitiveness	collaboration	enthusiasm
achievement	friendship	variety
control feelings to get job done	express inner feelings spontaneously even if they interfere with the job	allow for the full range of emotions to find expression
strive for upward mobility in jobs and social contacts	accept one's state in life; be resigned to one's fate; "go with the flow"	be all things to all people
"What do you do?"	"How are you?"	"What's next?"
self-esteem depends on how the world views our accomplishments	self-esteem depends on how the world views us	self-esteem depends on how many stages of development we have successfully maneuvered

The order: doing, being, being-in-becoming reflects the first, second, and third-order value preferences of mainstream U.S. citizens.

To illustrate,

1. How important is a job to the average American adult?

2. How does an adult respond when a job is unintentionally lost?

3. Which value (doing, being, or being-in-becoming) do your answers about a job highlight as primary?

4. How does the federal government explain its "go slow" approach to cleaning up the environment?

5. What do some Americans choose when the options are:

– saving an owl from extinction vs. having a job in the lumber industry?

– curtailing government spending to reduce the national debt and lower income taxes vs. continuing to have a job in the defense industry?

– voting to banish the sale of tobacco, a leading carcinogen, vs. continuing to have a job in the tobacco industry?

6. Assess your answers to the choices in question 5. Does "continuing to have a job" figure prominently in each case?

7. Would you agree that "having a job," a top-rated value among many Americans, confirms the American first-order preference for the value of "doing"?

Consider examples from another area of American life:

1. When you or a family member falls ill, what course of action is followed? List the steps:

2. When the family member who is ill visits the physician who identifies the malady and prescribes a therapy, what does this person do next?

3. Is it fair to say this family member cooperates with the suggested therapy? follows the proposed regimen until good health is restored?

4. What does the ill person do about "work"—whether at home or outside the home?

5. How long is the person "excused" from work?

6. What if the person delays in returning to work after regaining health? What is such a person called?

Your answers to these questions should illustrate how deeply Americans are committed to "doing." When afflicted with an illness, an American will "do" everything possible to "defeat" it. An ill person is temporarily excused from one kind of "doing," the major occupation, in order to engage in another kind of "doing": fighting the illness!

Notice also that the therapy also involves a plan and activities tailored to the plan with a view to gaining a very specific achievement: restoration to health.

7. How does an American react when the condition is not amenable to treatment? to therapy? (for example, a terminal disease or a life-long disability)?

8. Do you agree that when "doing" is not possible, the American will settle for "being"? settle for waiting until a miracle cure is discovered? for learning to live with the disability?

Finally, reflect upon the recent American interest in "holism." There is holistic health, holistic business management, and even holistic skiing.

1. Make a list of the situations in which you find the word "holistic" or situations in which you can recognize the reality behind the word "holistic" even if the word is not used?

2. Is your list long?

While the word and idea "holistic" is probably familiar to you, it is also likely that you do not hear it as often as you hear the word "job" or "work." This simple reflection may help you to recognize the validity of scientific observations about American value preferences. They are indeed: doing, being, and being-in-becoming in that order.

Now for one final consideration.

Do you think this same order of value preferences: doing, being, and being-in-becoming holds true equally for men and women?

Scholars observe that the dominant pattern of choices in each culture is generally not the same for men and women. In each culture, women generally are socialized for the second-order alternatives. Thus, the order of value preferences for *American middle-class women* is most often:

Being	Doing	Being-in-becoming

While American middle-class men are expected to "do" (planned activity geared toward achieving goals), American middle-class women are normally expected to "be"—that is, to deal with the husband's and children's feelings, to be primarily oriented toward spontaneous expression of her own feelings, etc.

While the American women's movement has made efforts to sensitize women and men to other options for women, the pattern of different value preferences appears still to remain generally unchanged. (See Carol Gilligan.)

Conclusion

Cultures differ among themselves mainly in the way they arrange their value preferences relative to basic human concerns. In regard to the basic challenge of determining a fundamental orientation toward human activity, the rank-order of value preferences among American, middle-class men is: "doing," "being," "being-in-becoming." At the same time, the rank-order of value preferences among American middle-class women is: "being," "doing," "being-in-becoming."

The situation is different in the ancient Middle East.

LESSON

The general, rank-order of value preferences in the first-century Mediterranean world is:

Being	Being-in-becoming	Doing

Refer to the chart above to review what is entailed when a culture's primary value orientation is toward "being." Then read the following passages with this preferred value orientation in mind:

Being

READ Matthew 11:16–19.

Jesus is directing a complaint to his Mediterranean listeners about their behavior.

> 1. Games, including children's games, reflect and reinforce the values of every culture. Here, Jesus refers to a game where children give "cues" to other children (Matthew 11:16–17).

What are the "cues"?

How do the other children respond to the cues?

Recall that "being" describes the value of responding spontaneously to challenges or "cues" in life. What spontaneous responses were expected in this game? What responses were actually given?

2. What "cue" did John the Baptist give for the game of life? (Matthew 11:18.)

How did his listeners respond?

Did they spontaneously respond to the cue, or did they resist the cue?

Did they behave according to the Mediterranean culture value preference of "being," or did they choose to momentarily suspend this value preference?

3. What cue did Jesus give for the game of life? (See Matthew 11:19.)

How did the listeners respond?

Did they spontaneously respond to the cue, or did they resist the cue?

4. Both John and Jesus are perceived as prophets. What is the significance of refusing to respond spontaneously to the cue of a prophet?

5. What then does Jesus mean by his concluding comment in verse 20 about "wisdom." What kind of "deeds" justify wisdom?

Do not be confused by the word "deeds." Remember how "doing" was defined above. It always involves careful planning and implementation with a view to achieving a goal. It does not include "spontaneous" behavior responding to the stimulus of the moment.

READ Matthew 12:1–8.

Reflect carefully on verse 1. Does the disciples' behavior manifest careful planning? Have they paused to consider the consequences of their action?

Would you agree that this illustrates yet again the primary value of "being," responding spontaneously to hunger pangs when they are felt?

READ Matthew 12:9–14.

Reflect carefully on verse 11. Does the owner of a sheep which has fallen into a pit pause to consider what day it is when his sheep is in danger of death?

Is this another illustration of the primary value orientation of "being," a spontaneous response to a potentially tragic situation?

READ Matthew 26:47–56.

Reflect carefully on verse 51. Consider this person carefully.

Why did he bring a sword along? Was it an ordinary item one carried around all the time?

It was already night when the supper ended, and in the garden Jesus went apart with three disciples to pray. What kind of person would strike out with a sword in a dark garden in which "a great crowd" armed with "swords and clubs" was now milling about?

Is this not a risky action? Is it perhaps even foolhardy?

Is not this action another illustration of the primary value orientation toward "being," that is, a spontaneous response to the situation at hand, a mob in a lynching mind-set?

These passages all record spontaneous actions undertaken without any consideration of their futility or their possible, unintended or undesirable consequences.

What of women in the New Testament?

READ Matthew 8:14–17.

1. What does Peter's mother-in-law do after the fever leaves her? (See verse 15.)

2. Why did Peter's mother-in-law not run out of the house and spread the good news of her healing, as such news was spread in Matthew 8:33; 9:26; 9:31?

3. Could one reason for her behavior lie in the distinctive ordering of values in which Mediterranean women are socialized: "doing," "being," "being-in-becoming"?

In other words, the mother-in-law is culture-bound to serve and wait upon males in the household.

Matthew's note that she served "Jesus" (instead of "them" as in Mark 1:31) also signals another Mediterranean cultural characteristic. The gift of healing, like every gift in the Mediterranean world, is not "free." A gift always entails a return. Jesus healed the mother-in-law; she immediately repays the favor by serving "him."

Scholars identify this as a "dyadic" contract (recall the previous lesson, section on Paul).

A dyadic contract is an informal and implicit, well understood arrangement whereby "you do me a favor, I do you a favor; now you owe me another favor, and I repay with a favor," endlessly... or until one of us calls a halt to it, usually by saying "thank you." True gratitude is demonstrated by repaying the favor, but never by saying "thank you."

In Mediterranean culture, saying "thank you" effectively says, "I will never need you again, so let me terminate this relationship now by saying 'thank you.'" "Thank you" ends the dyadic contract, a risky venture in a world where centralized government did not work to the advantage of the peasants who never knew when they would need a favor again. Hence the rarity of "thank you," and the frequency of doing and repaying favors. A common, Middle-Eastern saying asserts: "Don't thank me; you will repay me."

Being-in-Becoming

The second preferred value among Mediterranean natives after "being" is "being-in-becoming." Look back to the chart above to review what this outlook entails.

Recall that a concern for "being-in-becoming" reflects a culture's concern for developing the entire human personality in all its aspects. In contemporary America, those who pursue "holistic" approaches would immediately say that this refers to the development of "body, soul, and mind," or "body and spirit," or some other such combination of elements. The situation is different in the Mediterranean world.

READ 1 Samuel 16:1–13.

1. Who does Samuel think is the Lord's choice? (See verse 6.)

2. What does God think of Samuel's perception? (See verse 7.)

3. Pay special attention to the concluding part of verse 7:

What does God see?

What do human beings see?

As the text indicates, Mediterranean natives are not at all introspective. Only God can know what goes on inside people. Human beings can know and judge only by externals. Does this help you appreciate why honor and shame are the core values of this culture?

Recall that honor is a *public* claim to worth and a *public* acknowledgment of that worth. It's all rather external, isn't it?

READ Matthew 9:1–8.

What does verse 4 tell us about Jesus?

In the light of 1 Samuel 16:7, to whose behavior is Jesus' ability similar? In this matter, is he like other human beings or is he like God?

What then are the "externals" by which Mediterranean natives make judgments about one another? Human, bodily organs, body parts!

People in the Semitic world simply did not perceive the human bodily organs the same way we do. In that culture, the individual person and the outside world with which that person interacts are described metaphorically by using parts of the human body as metaphors. In fact, the human body is divided into three symbolic zones based on organs and behaviors.

1. Zone One: heart-eyes. Westerners associate thought with the brain, but not so the people in the Mediterranean world. Human beings have hearts for thinking together with eyes that collect data for the heart.

2. Zone Two: mouth-ears. Humans have mouths for communicating along with ears that collect the communications of others.

3. Zone Three: hands-feet. Human beings use their hands and feet in their behavior.

In other words, in the Mediterranean world, human beings are viewed as consisting not of body, mind, and spirit, but rather of three mutually interpenetrating yet distinguishable symbolic zones for interacting with various environments: (1) the zone of emotion-fused thought (*heart-eyes*); (2) the zone of self-expressive speech (*mouth-ears*); and (3) the zone of purposeful action (*hands-feet*).

	BODILY PARTS	FUNCTIONS
Zone One:	heart/eyes	emotion-fused thought
Zone Two:	mouth/ears	self-expressive speech
Zone Three:	hands/feet	purposeful action

Two things should be noted. (1) Our Mediterranean ancestors in the faith did not consciously and explicitly think and express themselves in these specific terms. This sketch is a contemporary, non-Mediterranean explanation of data that is readily available in the Bible, beginning to end. (2) This pattern of thinking and expression by which human beings are assessed and reported in terms of three body zones symbolically interpreted can be traced in the biblical text by means of the consistency with which the sacred authors use their vocabulary.

Here is a list of the words a discriminating Bible reader should attend to in order to perceive these symbolic body zones just as our Mediterranean ancestors in the faith would have.

Zone of Emotion-Fused Thought:

Organ:
  heart-eyes, including eyelid, pupil.

Its activities:
  to see, know, understand, think, remember, choose, feel, consider, look at.

Nouns and adjectives pertaining to this zone:
  thought, intelligence, mind, wisdom, folly, intention, plan, will, affection, love, hate, sight, regard, blindness.

Equivalent in U.S. culture:
>   intellect, will, judgment, conscience, personality thrust, core personality.

Zone of Self-Expressive Speech:

Organ:
>   mouth-ears, including also tongue, lips, throat, teeth, jaws.

Its activities:
>   to speak, hear, say, call, cry, question, sing, recount, tell, instruct, praise, listen to, blame, curse, swear, disobey, turn a deaf ear to.

Nouns and adjectives pertaining to this zone:
>   speech, voice, call, cry, clamor, song, sound, hearing; eloquent, dumb, talkative, silent, attentive, distracted, etc.

Equivalent in U.S. culture:
>   self-revelation through speech, communication with others, a human being as listener who dialogues with others in a form of mutual self-unveiling.

Zone of Purposeful Action:

Organs:
>   hands-feet, including arms, fingers, legs.

Their activities:
>   to do, act, accomplish, execute, intervene, touch, come, go, march, walk, stand, sit; specific activities such as to steal, kidnap, commit adultery, build, etc.

Nouns and adjectives pertaining to this zone:
action, gesture, work, activity, behavior, step, walking, way, and specific activities; active, capable, quick, slow, etc.

Equivalent in U.S. culture:
outward human behavior, all external activity, human actions upon the world of persons and things.

To explore this second-order Mediterranean value of "being-in-becoming,"

READ Matthew 5–7.

1. In Matthew 5:21–48, Jesus illustrates how his disciples must surpass those like the scribes who specialize in "observing the commandments." Notice how Jesus expands the commandments' scope.

What symbolic body zone does killing belong to (5:21)?

What symbolic body zone does anger belong to (5:22)?

What symbolic body zone does an insult ("you fool") belong to (5:22)?

Does it seem to you that this prohibition of killing deals with one symbolic body zone, but Jesus expands the prohibition to include the other two symbolic body zones as well?

Is this a good illustration of a cultural concern for "being-in-becoming," that is, a holistic development of the human person in all symbolic body zones?

2. In criticizing pious practices which characterized the Pharisees (6:1–18) Jesus again resorts to the symbolic body zones.

Which symbolic body zone is involved in almsgiving (6:2–4)?

Which symbolic body zone is involved in prayer (6:5–6)?

Which symbolic body zone is involved in fasting (6:16–18)?

In each instance, whose "seeing" is important (6:4, 6, 18)?

What symbolic body zone does "seeing" belong to?

Jesus does not reject the practices peculiar to the two symbolic body zones involved in Pharisee piety. He rather suggests that they are aimed toward an inappropriate third "symbolic body zone," namely, that of human beings rather than that of God.

3. In Matthew 6:19–27, Jesus describes a righteousness that is suitable for disciples, one that would surpass that of the scribes and Pharisees (see 5:20). This righteousness, too, is described in terms of appropriate symbolic body zones.

In Matthew 6:19–7:6, which symbolic body zone is discussed?

verse 21 "treasure in the heart";

verse 22 "eye the lamp of the body";

verses 25 and 24 "anxiety";

7:1 "judging"—mouth? or heart?

7:2 "brother's eye."

In Matthew 7:7–7:12, which symbolic body zone is discussed?

verse 7 "ask."

In Matthew 7:13–27, which symbolic body zone is discussed?

verse 13 "enter";

verse 17 "bearing fruit";

verse 21 "do the will of the father."

Does each of these segments wherein Jesus describes the righteousness appropriate for his disciples pertain to a different symbolic body zone?

Has Jesus mentioned all three symbolic body zones?

Does this suggest that righteousness as understood by Jesus promotes the value of "being-in-becoming" for his disciples? the value of developing all three symbolic body zones of the human personality equally?

Finally, does the fact that this option is already available in the culture, but as a second choice, make Jesus "counter-cultural"?

Or does Jesus rather tend to promote a culturally available alternative, similar to a culture's different arrangement of values for men and for women?

Doing

The third-order value preference in Mediterranean culture is "doing." Keep in mind that "doing" always includes the idea of a careful plan calculating the kinds of activities or deeds that are necessary in order to attain a specific goal. With this in mind, please consider the following passages.

READ Matthew 7:21–27.

1. What is Jesus' view on qualifications for entering the kingdom of heaven? (See verse 21.)

2. What then of the claims made by "prophets" on that final day? (See verse 22.)

3. What do you deduce from Jesus' judgment on these "prophets" in verse 23?

4. How would you summarize Jesus' attitude toward "doing" in these verses?

5. If he is promoting "doing" is he urging an alternative to his culture's preference for "being"?

6. Would you call this counter-cultural? Or is Jesus simply promoting an alternative that is already avail-

able in the culture? Recall that Mediterranean women are socialized into "doing" as their primary value preference. Would you agree that Jesus seems to be counter-structural? that he rearranges the structure of his society's values?

READ Matthew 12:46–50.

1. Here Jesus redefines kinship. What new basis of kinship does Jesus propose? (See verse 12:50.)

2. Does this verse echo Matthew 7:21?

3. What do you think Jesus means by the phrase he repeats: "do the will of my Father in heaven"?

Does it sound like a calculated plan with a view to achieving a goal (the definition of "doing" offered above)?

Or does it sound like something else?

Have you any idea what this "something else" might be? That is, if "doing the will of God" does not consist in setting out a plan and designing activities to achieve the goal, what then is it?

Perhaps the following text may shed some light.

READ Matthew 26:30, 36–46.

1. What does Jesus pray in the garden? (See verses 39, 42, 44.)

2. How does this sentiment compare with Jesus' exhortation to "do the will of the Father"?

3. Can the "doing" in the garden scene be viewed in a passive way? Is it anything Jesus actually "does," or is it rather that he submits or yields to what others do to him?

4. How does this view of "doing" God's will compare with any other familiarity you might have with the Middle East. For instance, is this similar to the Muslim understanding of "doing the will of God" which is usually expressed in conversation by the frequent repetition of *inshallah*, that is, "if God wills it"?

One travel guide to Middle-Eastern countries observes that when a Muslim hails a cab and is recognized as a Muslim by the driver, the driver will ask: "Where to, if God wills it?" And the rider will reply: "Straight ahead for five blocks, if God wills it." The rider obviously intends to go further than five blocks, but does not reveal the full journey for two reasons. The driver only needs to know a bit at a time, and there is no telling how far God wills this traveller to actually go, so he goes by stages.

Remember: "Doing" means designing a plan and taking steps to achieve a goal. "Being" means spontaneously responding to a given situation even if it disrupts what has been going on until that time.

From these passages, one might conclude that in his ministry and preaching, Jesus tried to persuade his Mediterranean contemporaries that they needed to take more initiative in their lives. "Being," the spontaneous enjoyment of whatever happens in life is good, too, but it can render people complacent. Jesus tried to stir them out of complacency.

Jesus was not alone in this mission, nor was it unique to him. Throughout the Jewish scriptures, the chosen people needed to be reminded again and again to "Keep (i.e., to obey and fulfill) the commandments." The reason for the repeated reminders is that they were chiefly satisfied with having been "chosen." They had little interest in "doing." To be a "chosen people" is a good "state of being." But the tradition had to remind them—and us—that that isn't enough.

Notice, however, how strong culture is. After an energetic ministry of reminding people to "keep the commandments" and to "do the will of God," in other words urging his listeners to place new emphasis on the cultural alternative of "doing" as well as the cultural first choice of "being," when Jesus is faced with a crisis in his own life, he reverts to the cultural first choice: "being,"—spontaneously responding to the situation he faces. Crisis always causes one's basic values to stand out rather starkly. In his crisis, Jesus makes no effort to escape, to thwart his would-be captors, to stir up a diversion. His choice is quite in contrast with a middle-class American faced with a similar challenge. Jesus responds quite appropriately to his crisis by "being"; he responds with fear, apprehension, and a hope that someone else might come to his assistance (my father, a legion of angels, etc.).

Conclusion

With reference to preferred value orientations toward human activity, the Mediterranean world socialized men into this order:

Being	Being-in-becoming	Doing

Mediterranean women are socialized toward the same values but in this order:

Doing	Being	Being-in-becoming

Though experts agree on this general order of value preferences in Mediterranean culture, they also caution that the order changes in differing circumstances. Consideration of these circumstances will be left to the Follow-up.

FOLLOW-UP

1. Compare the order of value preferences concerning human activity among middle-class Americans with the order among Mediterranean peasants.

American Men:

American Women:

Mediterranean Men:

Mediterranean Women:

In view of the differences between Mediterranean and American value preferences, how can a modern believer strive to implement the Bible's value exhortations?

2. Would it help to answer this dilemma by recalling that Jesus' conclusion to the parable of the good Samaritan was: "Go and do likewise, or in like manner" (Luke 10:37) and not "Go and do the same thing"?

3. Read the mighty deeds of Jesus clustered in Matthew 8—9. Among the healings, were people restored to a state of "doing" or to an improved "state of being"? Explain your interpretation in terms of the Mediterranean order of value preferences.

4. It is important to note that the model presented in this session, as in all sessions, is very general. It accurately describes the Mediterranean cultural world in general. However, nobody lives in any world in general. Everyone lives in specific circumstances, and specialists are aware of that.

Here is a list of value preferences that seem to describe different groups that lived in the ancient Mediterranean world. Limiting your reading to Matthew's gospel, see if you can validate or confirm these proposals:

Jewish Peasants:

Being	Being-in-becoming	Doing

For example, what was the spontaneous response of the servants in Matthew 13:24–30?

What was the equally spontaneous response of the house-holder?

Jewish Elites (e.g., Sadducees):

Being-in-becoming	Being	Doing

For example, consider the Sadducee question in Matthew 22:23–33.

Pharisees:

Being	Doing	Being-in-becoming

For example, in Matthew 16:1–4, what does Jesus say about the ability of the Pharisees to respond spontaneously to what they see ("being")?

Jesus:

Being-in-becoming	Being	Doing

Review the sermon on the mount, Matthew 5–7.

Can you find additional examples for each category?

Resources

Ferraro, Gary P. *The Cultural Dimension of International Business.* Englewood Cliffs, N.J.: Prentice-Hall, 1990. Especially Chapter Five: "Contrasting Cultural Values," 92–118.

Gilligan, Carol P. *In a Different Voice.* Cambridge, Mass. and London: Harvard University Press, 1982. How the values of American women differ from those of American men, and how these differences lead to different decisions.

Gilmore, David D. *Honor and Shame and the Unity of the Mediterranean.* Washington, D.C.: American Anthropological Association, 1987.

Malina, Bruce J. *The New Testament World: Insights from Cultural Anthropology.* Atlanta: Westminster/John Knox Press, 1981.

Patai, Raphael. *The Arab Mind.* New York: Scribners, 1983 revised edition.

Pilch, John J. "Sports and Values," *New Catholic World* 229 (1986), 165–167.

Pilch, John J. "Reading Matthew Anthropologically: Healing in Cultural Perspective," *Listening: Journal of Religion and Culture* 24 (1989), 278–289.

Pilch, John J. "Marian Devotion and Wellness Spirituality: Bridging Cultures," *Biblical Theology Bulletin* 20 (1990), 85–94.

Spiegel, John. "An Ecological Model of Ethnic Families," pp. 31–51 in Monica McGoldrick, John K. Pearce, and Joseph Giordano, eds., *Ethnicity and Family Therapy.* New York/London: The Guilford Press, 1981.

Session Five

Values and Human Relationships

P aul and Silas were praying in prison at Philippi when an earthquake shook all the doors open. The jailer thought they had escaped, but instead he found Paul and Silas still there. In response to his question: "What ought I do to be saved?" they said: "Believe in the Lord Jesus, and you will be saved, you and all your household." After tending to the wounds of Paul and Silas, the jailer was baptized, with all his family.

(Acts 16:25–43)

This first-century story reminds me of my ethnic roots. In A.D. 966, when the pagan Duke Mieszko of Poland married the Catholic Princess Dabrówka of Bohemia, he and his courtiers were baptized, and quickly thereafter all of Poland was converted to Catholicism and baptized. Such *group* conversions were the norm until after the fifteenth century!

Incidents like this sound strange to American individualists. Each American is taught from youth to stand alone on two feet, to do one's own thing, to "be all that *you* can be," and so forth. Americans generally convert on an individual basis. In the U.S., it is rather rare that an entire family, much less an entire village, city, or state converts to anything.

Hear the Word! Book One, Session Five, focused on these two contrasting values, group-orientation and individualism, in its examination of the so-called "Individual" Psalms of Lament. In this session we broaden the consideration to include a spectrum of three values in human relationships: individualism, collectivism and hierarchism.

Preparation: American individualism

Lesson: Mediterranean group-orientation

Follow-up: Further reflections on cultural differences in human relationships

---

PREPARATION

Another basic human challenge which all cultures face is how individuals should relate to each other. There are three options, and each culture arranges the options differently. Thus, with regard to human relationships, groups can choose from:

Individualism—This value reflects a preference for autonomy rather than responsibility to any group. Like all cultural value options, training for individualism begins already from infancy as youngsters are encouraged to express their personal needs and opinions. Individuals are "inner directed."

Group-orientation or **collateral relationships**—This value does not deny or negate individualism but rather regards the well-being of the *group* as the guarantor of well-being for the individual. Individuals seek the welfare of the group above their own wishes or desires in the conviction that group well-being will contribute to their personal welfare. In group-orientation, individuals are "other-directed." Other-directed individuals take their cues from peers or from group pressures.

Lineal relationships or **hierarchical-orientation**—This value generally flourishes (1) under conditions of material scarcity to control aggression and competition, and (2) in emergency situations requiring instant and unquestioned obedience. It is also evident wherever the social structure is stratified. Thus, it is manifest in the military, in bureaucracies, and in tradition-directed cultures or segments of a culture.

Cultures differ in the way they arrange these choices. Here, then, is yet another key to understanding the scriptures with respect for their Mediterranean cultural context, particularly as the scriptures reflect a value arrangement that differs from that of mainstream (or middle-class) United States culture. In this preparation for this session on human relationships, we focus on the arrangement of choices that characterize mainstream U.S. or middle-class American culture.

INDIVIDUAL-CENTERED	GROUP-CENTERED	LINEAL-ORIENTED
egocentric identity	group-centric identity	tradition-, authority-centered identity
promotes independence	promotes interdependence	promotes obedience and respect
see the parts	see the whole	see the lineal sequence
autonomy from social solidarity	integration into social reality	find and maintain the right location in the social ladder or hierarchy
primary responsibility to self and individual potential	primary responsibility to others and development of the group	primary responsibility to authority or tradition, and being loyal to it
urges uniqueness	urges conformity	urges obedience
group membership results from a renewable contract	group membership results from one's inherited social and familial place in society; or accepting a call to a fictive-kin group	lineal membership results from genealogical pedigree, induction, seniority
behavior is governed by rights and duties determined by one's personal goals	behavior is dictated by the group's mores and sanctions	behavior is dictated by tradition and/or authority
individual worth is based on individual achievements or individual possessions	individual worth is rooted in familial status or group status	individual worth is rooted in social position, class, caste, rank, etc.

status is achieved	status is ascribed	status is ascribed: inherited or merited
achieving and competing are motivational necessities and the norm	achieving and competing are disruptive; interdependent collaboration is the norm	vaunting one's prominence and authority is the norm
assert one's own rights	submit personal rights to the group	rights are delegated by authority or derived from the blood-line
equality is a key value	relative equality is a key value	hierarchy is a key value
friendships are functional	friendships involve long-term loyalties or obligational commitments	friendships are restricted to one's class, caste, rank, etc.
any group is viewed as only a collection of individuals	any group is viewed as an organismic unit, inextricably interlocked	any group is viewed as a hierarchically stratified organization mappable on a genealogy or flow-chart
the individual self is viewed as an entity separate from the physical world and from other persons	the individual self is viewed as organically connected with the physical world and with other persons	the individual self is viewed as hierarchically connected and appropriately located and subordinated in the physical world and with other persons

personal decisions are made by the self alone even if not in the group's best interests	personal decisions are made in consultation with the group and often in obedience or deference to its will	personal decisions are rooted in blind obedience to authority or deferential respect to tradition
private autonomy	corporate solidarity	linear discrimination: ethnocentrism, racism, sexism, and other "isms" based on real or imagined hierarchical ordering of values
strong personal identity	strong familial or fictive-kin identity	strong caste, class, ethnic, or other similarly lineal identity
strong desire to be personally satisfied	strong desire to be interpersonally satisfying or satisfactory	strong desire to mind one's place, honor superiors or ancestors, and to receive due respect
importance of personal time	importance of group needs	importance of tradition, the past
emotional independence from any group	emotional dependence upon the group	emotional fulfillment in the right group
involvements are calculative (individual values prevail)	involvements are moral (group values prevail)	involvements are restricted to what best serves tradition
key values are leadership and variety	key values are conformity and orderliness	key values are obedience and respect

other people are viewed in general terms (universalism)	other people are viewed in terms of competing factions, in groups and out groups (particularism)	other groups are viewed in terms of social status, standing, class (hierarchism)
greater degree of social mobility	lesser to no degree of social mobility	no need for social mobility
nuclear family structure predominates	extended family or tribal structures predominate	maintaining the family line predominates

Chart based on Pilch, *Hear the Word!* Book One, Session Five; David Augsburger and Geert Hofstede.

The order of values in the chart above: individual-centered, group-centered, and lineal-oriented reflects the first, second and third-order value preferences of middle-class Americans (or mainstream U.S. citizens).

To illustrate:

I. Individual-centered Orientation

Read and reflect upon the characteristics of this value orientation listed in the first column on the chart above.

How is this emphasis reflected in the way Americans view children and child-rearing?

Are middle-class American children trained toward individualism from an early age?

Consider these common American practices relative to child-care: use of baby-sitters; enrollment in pre-school or nursery school; permission to sleep over at the homes of friends; permission to travel without parents but with other friends and their parents on vacations; encouragement to move out and get an apartment after first getting a job; etc.

Do these practices encourage any of the values listed in the individual-oriented column?

Do these child-care practices leave parents more free to pursue their own self-interests? Does this favor individualism?

How would you interpret the oft-heard statement by elderly persons in television programs, commercials, and news stories: "I don't want to be a burden to my children"? Is that yet another reflection of the American value-preference for individual self-sufficiency?

In your own adult life, whether at home or at gainful employment, how many characteristics listed in the column of individual-oriented values can you identify?

II. Group-centered Orientation

American democracy was founded and relies upon a collateral orientation, or a group-centered orientation. Still, this value is a second-order choice, following upon a distinct preference for the individual.

Even the American family, a very fundamental group, is guided more by respect for the individual than by submission to the welfare of the group.

In "Human Life in Our Day" (November 1, 1968), the United States bishops wrote: "The present-day American family . . . is a community of individual persons joined by human love, and living a community life that provides for the greatest expression of individualism."

Is this true in your family as well?

Relative to groups other than the family, notice in the listings above that individualists hold that "group membership results from a renewable contract." American individuals join and support groups only insofar as the groups help the individual achieve personal goals: thus, weight-watchers, a computer support group, and other such groups are "second-order" choices for American individualists.

Make a list of groups you belong to (whether these be secular groups like clubs or labor unions; or religious like prayer groups or house-churches).

What motivated you to join the group?

How long have you belonged to the group?

How long do you intend to remain with the group?

Review the characteristics listed under the "group-centered" column in the chart above and identify those that pertain to the groups you have listed.

What advantages would a "small group" have over a "large group"?

How important is the "individual" in the above answer?

Do you think people of all cultures would answer this question in the same way?

From your knowledge of contemporary church experience, in which countries or cultures did "small groups" or "base communities" originate and flourish?

Might there be a cultural explanation for that?

Are those cultures primarily oriented toward individualism or are they primarily group-oriented?

III. Lineal Orientation (Hierarchical Orientation)

This is a very weak, third-order choice among mainstream United States citizens. It clearly is far removed from our primary emphasis on individualism. However, here are some instances where lineal-orientation values come into play in our culture.

High Society

If you have access to some of the major newspapers in the United States like *The New York Times*, *The Washington Post*, *The Los Angeles Times*, *The Chicago Tribune*, or perhaps even your local newspaper, read the section which announces engagements and weddings.

Here is a fictionalized composite:

> Mary Beth Smith, the daughter of Colonel and Dr. Howard J. Smith of St. James, L.I., N.Y., was married yesterday to Harold Maximillian Jones, a son of Mr. and Mrs. Bernard Jones of Ridgefield, Conn. The Reverend Seraphim J. Benedict officiated at Our Lady of Perpetual Consolation in Manhattan Beach, California.
>
> Ms. Smith, 28 years old, graduated cum laude from Boston College, and earned her M.B.A. at the University of Pennsylvania. She is an account executive with *Mysterium* magazine in New York. Her father is manager of career development at the I.C.B.M. Systems, a defense electronics company in Huntington, L.I. Her

mother is a law partner in the firm of Halsely and Lewis, Ltd., Manhattan.

The bridegroom, 31 years old, is an economist with Maintree and McGinnis, government bond dealers in New York. He graduated from St. Paul's School in Concord, N.H., and Princeton. He took a degree in jurisprudence from Oxford and received a law degree from Duke University. He is to join the Philadelphia law firm of Brinkley, Riddle and Heath in September. His father is a Circuit Court Judge for District 9. His stepmother is the president of Whizmore Financial Services in New York.

What kind of information is given about the bride and groom?

What kind of information is given about their parents and other significant relatives?

Does this information highlight "democratic equality" or does it rather point out a certain superior status?

How often do you read the social pages?

Who would read the social pages regularly?

How does the information contained on the social pages of a newspaper fit into a lineal or hierarchical orientation?

American Social Problems

Bureaucracy, ethnocentrism, and racism are social problems with roots in the value preference known as lineal-orientation. The fact that such third-order value preferences can flourish in a culture like that of the United States where the first-order value preference is for individualism and respect for individual worth indicates the powerful influence that even third-order value preferences can wield.

Bureaucracy

Does your organization have a flowchart?

Where do you fit in on the flowchart?

How does a person maneuver through the flowchart, either as a client seeking the right help, or as an employee in search of a promotion or career move?

Is it possible to skip boxes on the flowchart?

In a culture where the primary value orientation is on individualism, equality of persons and autonomy, what could possibly contribute to the flourishing of bureaucracies?

Could one possible explanation for bureaucracy be found in the values reviewed in the previous session: the American preference for "doing" and achieving?

One might think that the combination of "doing" and "individualism" as primary value orientations in a culture would produce a society overflowing with entrepreneurs, self-employed people, and the like.

How would you explain the willingness of so many people to express their "doing" (American first-order value preference) in a context governed by "lineal-orientation" (American third-order value preference) rather than in their own small business or as self-employed individuals?

Ethnocentrism
A certain amount of ethnic or national pride is natural and important in human relationships. Ethnocentrism occurs when a given culture or ethnic group tends to view the rest of the world's cultures and ethnic groups from its own perspective. "Why can't *they* be *like us*?" or "*They* are not as good as *we* are."

In the recent surge toward freedom in eastern Europe, did American television news-broadcasters tend to call this a move toward "democracy"?

Did it seem that the news-broadcasters assumed that there is only one kind of democracy, namely, the kind that exists in the United States?

Is it possible that hidden beneath these sentiments lies the attitude that American democracy is the best, the American way is the only way, American values the best values, etc.?

Did the observations sound a little like members of a given religious group claiming theirs is the "one, true way"?

Isn't it interesting that the American third-order value (a concern for lineal or hierarchical rankings) should overpower its first-order value (respect for individual autonomy, free choice, and the like) in international matters?

Racism

Racism is a clear example of prejudice and bias that is sometimes fostered and encouraged by the preference for lineal-orientation. Once the world can be stratified into groups of more or less value, then races are just another collection of groups to be similarly ranked.

The Thai culture values individualism as much as mainstream U.S. culture does. This in part explains the economic success of recent Thai immigrants to America. One might expect that people with similar values would be warmly received and accepted into a given culture.

Is this true of Thai people you are familiar with or have read about?

Everyone is familiar with the plight of the African-Americans in United States history. In Detroit, where African-Americans constitute the majority of the population, the Arabs and Arab-Americans are one of the ethnic minorities though their number there is larger than anywhere else in the U.S.

In Detroit and other parts of the United States, are Arabs and Arab-Americans ever the targets of racism or racist judgments?

Conclusion

Cultures differ among themselves in the way they arrange their value preferences relative to basic human concerns. Americans who aspire to read their Mediterranean-inspired Bibles should become very conscious of their own cultural values. This will help them recognize and respect the different, Mediterranean cultural values of their ancestors in the faith. In regard to the challenge of determining how to get along with others, the general, rank-order of value preferences among American, middle-class citizens is: individual-orientation; group-orientation; and lineal-orientation.

The value-orientation of the Bible concerning human relationships is quite different.

LESSON

The general, rank-order of value preferences in the first century Mediterranean world is:

Group-centered	Lineal	Individual

Notice that the first-order value preference of middle-class Americans (individualism) is the third-order value preference of first-century Palestinian peasants! This means that an American Bible reader should expect to find little or nothing of the common, daily, *American* experience of individualism in the Bible. Please refer to the chart above to review what is entailed in a culture's primary value orientation toward collateral relationships, or a group-centered focus.

As you read through Mark's gospel take note of (1) the value preferences, and (2) the groups or individuals characterized by the preferences.

I. Group-centered

In group-centered value orientations, remember that the individual's primary responsibility is to the group and the development of the group. Also recall that other people are viewed by group members as competing factions. Thus, in a group-centered society there are many in-groups and outgroups.

READ Mark 9:38–41.

Why did John forbid another person to cast out demons in Jesus' name (v 38)?

Which is the ingroup and which is the outgroup here?

What did Jesus respond (v 40)?

What does Jesus' statement reveal about his views on groups? his views on competition?

In the group-centered orientation, group membership results from birth or from a "call," a special invitation to join the group. Once a person joins the group, it is not easy to abandon it. In a group-centered culture, friendships involve long-term loyalties or obligational commitments

READ Mark 3:13–19.

Jesus summons a group in verse 13. What does he do next? Does he narrow the group down (v 14)?

Jesus is technically involved in faction-formation. A faction is a group centered around a leader. Those called respond because they believe in the leader's cause and are willing to join him in obtaining that cause. At the same time, all those called have weak common bonds to each other, with some exceptions.

READ Mark 1:16–20.

How are Simon and Andrew related (v 16)?

How are James and John related (v 19)?

What would prompt these two sets of brothers to drop everything and follow this perfect stranger?

READ Mark 3:31–35.

Who comes calling upon Jesus (v 31)?

How does Jesus respond (vv 32–33)?

Group-orientation most definitely includes attachment to one's family, a very basic group in every culture no matter how family is defined. What does this passage suggest about Jesus' attachment to his family?

Can Jesus be viewed in these verses as reinterpreting or redefining family?

Does this make him counter-cultural or is he rather proposing a different structure of relationship?

Is he offering an option that would destroy the culture, or is he offering an option which is already available in the culture: namely, joining groups?

If Jesus simply offers an alternative, then is he counter-structural but not counter-cultural on this point?

Group-centered orientation promotes interdependence. Group members have a primary responsibility to others in the group. Competition by individual group members is viewed as disruptive, while interdependent collaboration is the norm.

READ Mark 10:35–45.

What do James and John request of Jesus (v 37)?

How do the other ten feel about that (v 41)?

What does an appreciation of group-centered orientation contribute to the understanding of this passage?

How is the behavior of James and John similar to or different from behavior in the American corporate world? or in any part of American culture?

READ Mark 2:1–12.

Who brought the paralytic to Jesus? (See verse 3.)

Who brought the sick to Jesus in Mark 1:32–33?

Is this an illustration of group interdependence?

READ Mark 1:30–31.

What does Simon's mother-in-law do after the fever leaves?

Does this illustrate the greater importance of group needs over personal needs?

READ Mark 7:1–13.

Which two groups stand in conflict here (vv 1–5)?

What do the Pharisees complain about (v 2)?

Notice the Pharisee concern about the "tradition of the elders." Does their group-orientation appear to involve an element of lineal-orientation?

What does Jesus attack (vv 9–13)?

Is the "corban" a "pro-family" or an "anti-family" custom?

In the light of group-orientation or lineal-orientation values, how would you assess a group that proposes "corban" as an approved practice?

In all these illustrations of group-orientation, note well how individual needs are subordinated to group needs. Read over the list of characteristics under group-orientation in the chart above to attain a strong grasp of this value preference. It fairly well dominates the scriptures, as one would expect in Mediterranean culture.

II. Lineal Orientation

About 95 percent of the first-century Palestinian population were peasants. Peasants definitely favor their family above all, and then the village. Group-orientation is a primary value. At the same time, they are obligated to the landowners as well as to authorities, but this is not their primary concern or motive for behavior. Hence, lineal-orientation, or hierarchical concern, is a second-order value preference for the peasantry. At the same time, lineal-orientation is a first-order value for the elite and authorities in this same world.

READ Mark 11:27–33.

What is the question posed to Jesus (v 28)?

Who would be agitated over respect for or disregard of "authority"? peasants? or elites (v 27)?

What is Jesus' response (v 33)?

Is there a difference in value-orientation between Jesus and those who asked him the question?

Does their respective social status have a bearing on the relative importance each would attribute to concern about authority?

READ Mark 12:13–17.

What is the question posed to Jesus (v 14)?

What kind of people are concerned with "lawful" and "unlawful" behavior? ordinary people? or specialists in the law (v 13)?

What is Jesus' response (v 17)?

What side does Jesus seem to come down on?

READ Mark 9:33–37.

What were the disciples discussing on the way (v 34)?

Does this discussion flow from a group-orientation or a lineal-orientation?

How does Jesus view the topic under discussion (v 35)?

Does his advice tally with any characteristic listed in the chart above under group-orientation?

Jesus would certainly seem to be group-oriented and quite opposed to a lineal-orientation.

Thus, lineal-orientation does enter into the lives of all people in this culture. For some, like the elite, this consideration is primary. For others, like the peasant majority, hierarchies do indeed govern their lives but their primary focus is collateral, to their family and village.

III. Individualism

It is important to distinguish individual*ism* from individu-al*ity*. Individualism is a self-concept in which the person directs all motivations and behaviors to the achievement of individual goals without regard for any group, including the family. In contrast, individuality is the freedom of a person to express many different aspects of the self in different and various contexts. Even cultures like the Mediterranean, where stereotyping is a common strategy, recognize traits of individuality. The impetuous Peter is certainly unlike John; Jesus is not like the Baptist; Mary the mother of Jesus is not like Herodias.

Individualism is strikingly weak and mostly lacking in the Bible and the biblical world.

Make a list of the people Jesus healed:

Mark 1:32

1:40

2:3

3:1

3:10

5:2

5:25

7:32

8:22

10:46

What are their names?

Does this information surprise you?

Where do these people live, or where did they come from?

If you were to look for their graves, how would you find them?

Does it seem to you that even the individuality of these people healed is somewhat blurred?

The rarity with which people are identified by name in the New Testament confirms that individualism or individual-orientation is a third-order value in Mediterranean culture. A corollary to this is stereotyping: to know one leper is to know them all. No need to know individual names.

Male a list of all the Pharisees in Mark's gospel:

Mark 2:16

2:18

2:24

3:6

7:3

7:5

8:11

8:15

10:2

12:13

Are any identified by name?

Do the comments and context of these passages present information about individuals or about a group?

Make a list of all the individuals mentioned and identified by name in Mark:

Do any of the characteristics of individual-orientation listed in that column on the chart above seem to apply to these instances?

As best as you can determine, what social class do the named individuals represent: peasants? elite?

Do the individuals named merely illustrate how the group to which they belong ordinarily behaves?

READ Mark 8:34–38.

How do you read and interpret Jesus' instructions (vv 34–37)?

Do these sound as if they are directed to individuals?

Are these individuals being advised to stand alone, make a personal decision, resist any and all pressure?

What is the significance of the introduction to verse 34?

To whom has Jesus addressed this individualistic-sounding advice?

Does it seem that Jesus is concerned about a group, his followers?

Does the advice seemingly given here to individuals resonate with any of the characteristics of group-orientation on the chart above?

Note: Individualism is such a strongly affirmed cultural value among middle-class Americans that it is often perceived where in fact it doesn't exist. Sometimes such perception is called "ethnocentrism," that is, a tendency to view others as if they were culturally identical with those who are doing the viewing.

American Bible readers may well think they see individualism in Mediterranean texts where it is actually absent. The best advice is to become as familiar as possible with the list of characteristics presented for each value-orientation on the chart.

Conclusion

In general, the rank-order of value preferences that characterize the first-century Mediterranean world is:

Group-centered	Lineal-centered	Individualism

These value-preferences can be arranged differently by different groups in a culture (e.g., Pharisees, Herodians,

Sadducees, the Jesus-group, farmers, etc.) as well as by group members under specific circumstances (e.g., Jesus-group members James and John). We shall pay more attention to this in the follow-up section.

FOLLOW-UP

The great usefulness of this model for analyzing and comparing value preferences within a culture as well as across cultures is that it allows an observer to attend to many nuances and peculiarities. In every culture, there is a prevailing and preferred arrangement of value preferences, and there is also an alternative arrangement preferred by other groups and sometimes even by individual members of those groups.

As was evident above, the Pharisees, concerned with the traditions of the elders, would seem to prefer this arrangement:

Lineal-centered	Individual	Group-centered

The Jewish elite, e.g., Herod, his family and court, as well as many Sadducees would prefer this arrangement:

Lineal-centered	Group-centered	Individual

Some scholars have suggested that Jesus' value preferences as deduced from his representation in the gospels might be:

Group-centered	Individual	Lineal-centered

Readers might select one or another of these groups just mentioned, review the characteristics listed in the chart at the beginning of this session, and then reread Mark's gospel to explore the validity of the proposed arrangement as well as to note differences from the proposed arrangement.

At the same time, American Bible readers may appreciate taking another close look at American culture. In general, American middle-class value preferences are:

Individual	Group-centered	Lineal-centered

The same Americans who cherish individualism and individual initiative and free choice willingly accept and adopt quite a different arrangement of value preferences when they serve in the military:

Lineal-centered	Group-centered	Individual

Military history is replete with stories of individuals who saved the platoon, often at the price of their own life. There are times and circumstances when value preferences are adjusted.

Some Americans have even taken to living in communes, or have joined end-of-the-world groups and taken refuge in mountain or cave hideouts to ride out the coming storm. The value-orientation here may be:

Group-centered	Lineal-centered	Individual

One might believe that such groups are primarily lineal-centered since they often willingly pay blind obedience to their visionary leader.

In general, the prevailing value preferences for each

culture as identified by specialists is widely accepted and agreed upon. The general Mediterranean arrangement of value preferences is the opposite of the general American arrangement of value preferences. This is an important guideline for reading scripture with respect for its cultural setting.

The nuances possible in each culture are also enlightening.

In the long run, the Bible reader interested in bridging American and Mediterranean cultures needs to understand both well and apply the appropriate corrective. In general, Jesus sometimes seemed to have proposed an individual emphasis to stir his contemporaries from hiding behind the group. In general, Americans sometimes need to be sensitized to group needs lest they become totally blinded by individualism. No choice is a wrong choice, but all choices can be regularly examined for balance from time to time.

Resources

Augsburger, David W. *Pastoral Counseling Across Cultures.* Philadelphia: Westminster, 1986. Especially Chapter 3: "Individualism, Individuality, and Solidarity: A Theology of Humanness," pp. 79–110.

Hofstede, Geert. *Culture's Consequences: International Differences in World-Related Values.* Abridged Edition. Beverly Hills/London/New Dehli: Sage Publications, 1984. Especially Chapter 5: "Individualism," pp. 148–175.

Pilch, John J. *Hear the Word!* Book One, Session Five.

Pilch, John J. *Christian Families.* Dubuque, IA: W.C. Brown/ROA filmstrips.

Session Six

Values and Time Orientation

During a recent trip to Italy, the travel-package that my wife and I purchased included a Flexi-Pass for the railroad. We were entitled to four days of first-class, reserved-seat travel within nine days of validating the pass.

We planned our days carefully and stood in long lines at the railway station to make our reservations for the days and specific trains on which we wanted to travel from one city to another.

When we travelled by train, we noticed that Italian travellers who came to our compartment did not have any reservations. They sat where they pleased, dumped their abundant luggage in other vacant seats, and had loud and lengthy discussions with the conductor when he came to collect tickets. Not only did these travellers not have reservations, they hadn't even bought tickets! They paid a hefty "supplement" to the fare (a penalty) for purchasing the tickets on the train instead of in advance.

This experience highlighted a key difference in time orientation between Mediterranean (Italian) and western (United States) culture.

Americans are primarily *future-oriented*. Americans invented future-planning! Americans plan ahead, make reservations, take out insurance policies relative to future eventualities that may never occur (fire, accident, failed health, etc.). Americans are so future-oriented they firmly believe that *youth* is the future of America, even though the 85-year-old and older age cohort is presently the fastest growing sector of the American population. In the year 2080 this cohort is projected to constitute 25 percent of the population, while the 18-year-old and younger age cohort is projected to shrink from its present 25 percent to 17 percent of the population.

Mediterranean cultures do not give much consideration to the future. Instead, they are primarily *present-oriented*. People in the Mediterranean world give little thought on Monday to what they might want to do on Friday or that week-end. When they decide on an activity, they up and do it. Hence the families we encountered on trains who boarded with no ticket and no reservation.

Recall Jesus' Mediterranean advice in the gospel:

> Don't worry about what you will eat, or about what you will wear. Life is more than food and clothing. (Luke 12:22)

This very *present-oriented* observation follows the parable about the man who had a bumper crop and planned to build bigger barns in which to store it *for the future*. Jesus' remark is clearly a *criticism of future-orientation*. In his Mediterranean world, only God knows the future. Human beings should not waste precious *present time* by worrying about the future.

Recall Jesus' other Mediterranean comments that reflect a similar present-time orientation and disregard the future:

> But of that day or that hour *no one knows*, not even the angels in heaven, nor the Son, but only the Father. (Mark 13:32)

> It is not for you to know the times or seasons which the Father has fixed by his own authority. (Acts 1:7)

In this session, we shall focus on value differences between Mediterranean culture and middle-class American culture based on distinctive and contrasting time orientations or time preferences.

Preparation: The American primary orientation toward the future

Lesson: The Mediterranean primary orientation toward the present

Follow-up: Further contrasts of time orientation

PREPARATION

Yet another basic human challenge which all cultures face is how to orient themselves toward time. Once again, there are three options in each culture, but each culture arranges the options differently. The question can be posed in this way: When people are confronted with a vital problem, do they turn initially toward the past, the present, or the future for a solution? A second question is: Which of these options serves as a backup if the preferred option does not work? Here is an explanation of each option relative to time orientation:

The present—This value reflects a preference for the moment, for achieving proximate goals. Immediate needs and desires are of utmost importance. If hungry now, I pluck and eat mature ears of corn in the field right now without taking any thought of possible, future consequences of this action (Luke 6:1–5). The present orientation attends to the current moment understood in a wide sense to include even tomorrow but nothing beyond that (see Luke 11:3). This time orientation favors a group focus since in the present moment every member of the group stands an equal chance of addressing the present challenge and determining the proper response to the present opportunity.

The past—This time orientation looks to the past as a basic orientation. How did the ancestors respond? What did they accomplish and what status did they hold? In this orientation, the past is a guide and source of wisdom for the present which cannot surpass the past. In many cultures, elites are past-oriented since that is where their claim to elite status originated. Hence the concern among elites about pedigree, roots, and genealogies. This time orientation also respects the elderly as major repositories of wisdom.

The future—This time orientation believes anything new is better than anything old. The future will always surpass the present and the past. Future-oriented cultures set future-oriented goals, achievable at some future date, like becoming a college professor, an astronaut, a physician, etc. This time orientation cherishes youth as the promise of the future.

In this matter of time orientation, once again cultures differ in they way they arrange their choices. Time orientation, then, is still another key to understanding scripture. By paying due attention to the time orientation peculiar to Mediterranean culture, a Bible reader can read the text with greater respect and sensitivity. Readers should not be surprised to see reflected in the scriptures a time orientation that is quite different from that of the mainstream, United States culture. In the preparation for this session on time orientation, we focus on the arrangement of choices that characterize middle-class American culture.

FUTURE ORIENTATION	PRESENT ORIENTATION	PAST ORIENTATION
tends to locate goals in the extended or distant future	tends to seek goals and objectives in the present	seeks to measure up to the past but not to surpass it
activity occurs in the present to achieve remote, distant goals	activity occurs in the present to enjoy the present and achieve proximate goals	activity occurs in the present to sustain and glory in past achievements
time is a unit of impersonal value, like numbers on a digital clock	the extended present is a unit of personal expression	the past is a treasure-trove of wisdom, status, and achievement which shapes present identity
the distant future is continuous with the present	proximately forthcoming events are continuous with the present	distant past events are memorialized and influence the present
personal control is part of the cause and effect of future outcomes	there is no personal control over the proximate outcomes	the past ought to guide and mold the present; personal responsibility is to respect the past
cognitive, individualistic focused processes dominate future-oriented behavior	affective, group-focused processes dominate present-oriented behavior	affective, group-focused processes determined in the past guide present behavior
future can be shaped by individuals	individuals must guard the precarious present from which the forthcoming emanates	individuals must preserve the past as the only sure guide for success in the present

the future drives and propels the present	the present drives and propels the forthcoming	the past drives and propels the present
feedback for future-oriented people comes from realizing proximate goals and concerns knowledge of the status of future-goal achievement	feedback for present-oriented people derives from immediate social interaction and concerns present survival and positive affective support	feedback for past-oriented people derives from successful maintenance of the status quo and concerns the respect awarded from like-minded for this achievement

Chart adapted and expanded from Bruce J. Malina, "Christ and Time: Swiss and Mediterranean?" *Catholic Biblical Quarterly* 51 (January 1989), 8–9.

The order of values in the chart above—future, present and past orientation—reflects the first, second and third-order value preferences of middle-class Americans (or mainstream U.S. citizens).

To illustrate:

I. Future orientation

Read and reflect upon the characteristics listed in column one on the chart above.

In your youth, how did parents, teachers, and other significant adults guide you toward future vocation or career choices?

Were these short-range choices? or a series of choices geared toward a far-off goal: Harvard? law or medical school? a military career?

How much time do you now spend thinking and planning for the future?

Do you have investments for retirement? the education of your family?

Have you been successful in your future planning?

Though Americans are future-oriented and have honed future-planning to a science, evidence does not necessarily indicate they do it well.

On May 15, 1956, the General Motors Technical Center at Warren, MI., buried a time capsule under its front lawn with copies of two local newspapers, letters from three presidents of universities in Indiana and news releases about the capsule.

The capsule was unearthed on the 25th anniversary of its burial in 1981.

Car plans drawn in 1956 by GM engineers anticipating 1981 models were much more elaborate and were calculated to use more fuel than the actual 1981 models.

The three university presidents: Herman B. Wells of Indiana U., Frederick Hovde of Purdue U., and the Rev. Theodore Hesburgh of Notre Dame U., were much more on target than the car drawings but were inaccurate in other significant ways.

The university presidents underestimated by substantial amounts the real economic growth of the U.S. in twenty-five years (1956 to 1981), but overestimated the speed with which certain technological development would occur.

Interestingly, none of the presidents made any mention of the women's movement or the impact of the movement of women into the work force which moved up from 66.5 million in 1956 to 106 million in 1981.

None of the presidents even hinted at space flight to the moon, or the space age accomplishments that have become commonplace in our age.

A similar report can be made for the city of Milwaukee, WI. The local history collection at the Milwaukee Public Library holds an artist's conception drawn in 1910 of what Milwaukee would look like in the year 2010. It was published in the *Greater Milwaukee Magazine*.

City residents of that time commonly boasted that Milwaukee had a harbor superior to the Bay of Naples. Accordingly, the artist's drawing of Milwaukee in the year 2010 depicts a harbor at the end of Wisconsin Avenue filled with gondolas. Dirigibles are tied up at skyscrapers which approximate the height of those currently familiar to us, but these skyscrapers all have the architectural features of 1910!

Experts point out that there are two ways of forecasting the future: a linear view, and a "steps of discontinuity" approach. Both examples above seem to reflect the linear view. If this is what happened as a result of the preceding x-number of years, then we can expect this to happen in the next x-number of years.

"Steps of discontinuity" is a more difficult approach, for here the prognosticator tries to identify major events that will occur to change the future: e.g., oil shortages; a powerful women's movement; space travel and its concomitant scientific discoveries.

Even with an awareness of these difficulties and shortcomings, a future-oriented culture like the mainstream U.S. will continue to maintain its future perspective.

II. Present orientation

When middle-class Americans are thwarted in their future orientation, their next favorite orientation is present orientation.

For instance, when a plunge in the value of stocks or real estate suddenly darkens an investor's picture of the future, does attention revert rather quickly to the present?

– How much do I have left?

– What do I do now?

Notice how closely connected a present orientation is to a sense of having no control over events. Peasant populations in general are all present-oriented. With only a primitive knowledge of meteorology, irrigation, fertilization, crop rotation, etc., the focus must necessarily be on "today" over which they realize they have no control.

Proximate goals: Present-oriented people focus on proximate objects and goals.

Do Americans choose proximate goals as such?

Or are these proximate goals more often than not connected in some way with an ultimate, future goal or object?

For instance, it used to be a custom for people to initiate an annual, weekly-saving plan called "The Christmas Club." A person would estimate the amount of money needed to purchase gifts next year and would put aside a set amount each week to attain that sum. Clearly, saving a set amount of money each week is a proximate goal. But this proximate goal is directed to the ultimate goal of the final sum which could then be withdrawn and spent for gifts, the real purpose behind all this saving activity.

Forthcoming events in the present: Present-oriented people have no time to waste on the future. Anything that outsiders might consider "future" is to the present-oriented person an item coming forth from the present.

The imminent death of a person with a diagnosed terminal disease illustrates a "forthcoming event in the present." The death is already present in the existing terminal disease. This, of course, is a rather western example, since contemporary medical scientists can predict imminent death with greater certainty than can be done in primitive situations.

In the peasant context, the pregnancy of a mother is a forthcoming event which is viewed as already present given all the signs of pregnancy.

III. Past orientation

Early in his presidency, George Bush, an American World War II veteran, made reference in a speech to Pearl Harbor, and identified the date as *September* 7, 1941.

Of course this was a slip of the tongue, and no doubt behind it was a momentary lapse of memory. History records that the Japanese attack on Pearl Harbor took place on *December* 7, 1941.

Even so, anyone who has ever taught middle-class

students in the United States has sooner or later noticed that "history" for them appears to begin with the year of their birth.

From that time forward, they tend to count years in decades: the 60s, the 70s, the 80s, the 90s.

Events that occurred before the birth of these middle-class American students is usually confused and lost in a haze called "the past."

The past is generally not well known by Americans, including the past of their own families. The novel and film *Roots* inspired a passing interest in family history and genealogies which persists in some pockets of the population but quickly died out in the general American population.

The prevalent future orientation of Americans tends to belittle the past, to view it as "prologue." The future will always be better, so why bother with the past?

Summary

This brief overview of American value preferences relative to time orientation is intentionally sketchy and intended mainly to prepare the reader for encountering a vastly different time orientation in reading New Testament documents from the ancient, Mediterranean world.

LESSON

The general, rank-order of value preferences relative to time orientation in the first century Mediterranean world is:

Present	Past	Future

Notice that the *first*-order value preference of middle-class Americans (the future) is the *last*-order value preference among Mediterranean peasants! This means that an American Bible reader can expect to find very little if any of the typical American future orientation and concerns in the Bible. Review the chart above once more to see what is entailed in a culture's primary value orientation toward the present as its basic temporal orientation.

I. The Present

Recall the experience of my wife and myself on Italian trains recounted at the beginning of the chapter. We middle-class Americans pride ourselves on being responsible individuals who keep a keen eye on the future.

Though "normal" for Americans, this future orientation as a primary or secondary preference was and still is, in the opinion of cultural specialists, extremely rare on this planet. Peasant societies, such as that mirrored in our New Testament texts, are primarily present-oriented.

READ these passages reflecting Jesus' typical Mediterranean outlooks:

Luke 9:27

Luke 21:32

Since the people in those scenes did indeed die, what are we to make of these passages?

Was Jesus speaking like a typical, present-oriented, Mediterranean person of his time and place?

How have you previously read and interpreted these passages and their contexts?

How have they been presented to you in preaching?

Does an appreciation of Mediterranean time preference contribute to a better understanding of these passages?

READ Luke 12:13–34.

What is the legitimate request made to Jesus by one of the crowd (Luke 12:13)?

It was and still is very honorable in the Mediterranean world to be selected as a *mediator* in a dispute. A mediator must be removed at least by five degrees of kinship with the parties in a dispute. Here it seems as if Jesus is a total stranger.

The mediator's role is critical because of the constant risk of disputes escalating to violence and even bloodshed. Mediterranean people readily enter into disputes since they know they can always count on a mediator to intervene and save the day. Disputing, you will recall, is part and parcel of an honor-and-shame culture. It is a strategy for gaining honor and shaming another. (See *Hear the Word!* Book One, Session Three: Core Cultural Values.)

Jesus refuses the invitation (Luke 12:14). What excuse does he offer (v 15)?

"Covetousness, greed" is a cardinal failure in peasant societies. These people believed that all goods were finite in number and already distributed. Mediterranean peasants believe "there's no more where this came from." Once it's lost or spent, it's gone forever. In contrast, middle-class Americans believe "there's always more (money, oil, food, etc.) where this came from."

While the request to Jesus was to "divide" the inheritance, Jesus wonders if one of the brothers isn't trying to get "more" than the other. Hence his suspicion of greed.

Jesus then follows this warning against greed with the parable of the man with the bumper crop (Luke 12:16–21).

How do you interpret the parable?

Did the man with the crop behave prudently, correctly, from your middle-class American perspective?

Doesn't it make sense for an American—for *any* person—to plan for the future?

Why does God call this man who plans for the future a "fool" (v 20)?

What is God's criticism?

What is wrong with "laying up treasure for oneself" (v 21)?

In the Mediterranean world, anyone who suddenly increased his possessions was suspected of doing it at the expense of another or others. Thus, a landowner with a sudden, bountiful harvest—all worked out by nature!—is still suspected of depriving others of what belongs to them.

The landowner's proper course of action should be a *present-oriented solution*. He should immediately distribute the surplus to all who are in need.

Hence,the obvious meaning of Jesus' observation in verse 22.

Why should one not worry about what one will eat? Because those with a surplus are expected to share, now, in the immediate present.

Notice that the landowner who experienced this bountiful harvest is described as "rich" (v 16). Recall that just a few verses earlier Jesus warned the petitioner, a prospective heir, to beware of all "greed" (v 14). When reading the Bible, and especially the New Testament, it is a good idea to replace the word "rich" with the word "greedy." It is not the rich as such whom Jesus scolds, but rather the greedy, those who refuse to share their surplus. Surely this idea is familiar to anyone who follows contemporary Middle Eastern stories of oil-wealth carefully.

In Jesus' parable, the "rich" landowner who preferred to hoard his surplus crops rather than share them immediately turned out to be "greedy." That is how his culture—and Jesus—judged him, even though in our middle-class American eyes, he simply initiated an "I.R.A." (Individual Retirement Account).

READ Luke 18:28–30.

What is the reward for those who make sacrifices for the kingdom of God (v 30)?

When will they receive this reward (v 30)?

What do you understand by "the age to come" (v 30)?

Does Luke 9:27 and 21:32 help you to see that "the age to come" is "forthcoming from the present," sort of just around the corner, part of a rather wide understanding of a present?

READ Luke 11:2–4.

Does the petition regarding "bread" reflect a present or a future orientation (v 3)?

Some scholars translate this verse: "Give us today our bread for tomorrow." Is this a future orientation or is tomorrow normally included by Mediterranean people in the present?

In summary, an attentive reading of the Bible highlights the prevailing present orientation throughout the texts. This present orientation is also connected to other Mediterranean values we have examined: "being," a spontaneous response to the present moment; and "group-orientation," a concern for the group—family, extended family, village, etc. Every culture's arrangement of values is intimately connected to form a whole. To touch or disturb one value disturbs them all. This is why it is difficult to attempt to run counter to any culture.

II. The Past

Ordinarily, peasants never feel sufficiently liberated from the cares of the present to be concerned about anything else, past or future. Thus, for peasants the past is a secondary time orientation. Elites, however, and others with high status would be primarily oriented toward the past when their status was determined because the security of their present was pretty much guaranteed by that past.

READ Luke 3:1–9.

What kind of time orientation is presented as the context for John the Baptizer's ministry (vv 1–2)?

Are you able to identify the "relational" dimension of time in situating John in his proper temporal context?

What is more important here: knowledge of a calendar, or knowledge about personalities and which personalities were contemporary with one another?

How does the Baptizer attack the complacency of some who come to be baptized by him (v 8)?

Can pride in having Abraham as an ancestor become excessive and deluding?

Would you consider such pride an illustration of potentially excessive interest in the past and insufficient attention to the present?

Notice verse 7 (fear of the wrath to come) and verse 9 (the axe is being wielded *now*). Does this coupling of verses help you to grasp our ancestors' view of the "future" as immediately forthcoming from the present?

In other words, is the "future" far off in the distance or right around the corner, right now?

READ Luke 6:1–11.

Here are a couple of reports set on the sabbath.

How does Jesus defend his disciples' present action in the cornfield (vv 3–4)?

Would you agree that Jesus believes it is much more important to satisfy present hunger than to revere a tradition rooted in the past?

How do you assess Jesus' self-justification for healing the man with the withered hand on the sabbath (vv 6–9)?

How do you assess the scribes and the Pharisees (vv 7, 11)?

Is it fair to say they cherish the past as a primary value orientation and the present as a secondary value orientation?

Does Jesus hold exactly the opposite view?

In this matter is Jesus counter-cultural, or is he rather counter-structural, that is, he arranges his priorities like a peasant and not like a member of the elite?

III. The Future

A biblical scholar who specializes in the Mediterranean cultural context of the Bible has noted:

> There surely is no expressed concern for the future in the Synoptic story line. And it would appear that the same holds for the entire New Testament since any time description consisting of this age and a rather proximate age to come has no room for a future of the sort we speak of. To what then would New Testament prophecies refer? Did they in fact refer to the future or to the present? Is the presumed future orientation seen to underpin such prophecies actually derived from the Bible or is it the product of rather recent experience?
> (Malina, *Christ and Time*, p. 7)

To explore the validity of this observation, read over the entire gospel of Luke and make a list of "future" references, future in the sense as described on the chart above. This means a future far removed from this present, but certainly capable of being managed and shaped by present actions.

READ these "Son of man" passages in Luke.

As one possible focus, consider these references to "Son of man" in Luke, and identify the passages where you find a reference to someone who will be coming at some time in the very distant future.

5:24

6:5

6:22

9:22

9:26

9:44

9:58

11:30

12:8

12:10

12:40

17:22

17:24

17:26

17:30

18:8

18:31

19:10

21:27

21:36

22:22

22:48

22:69

24:7

Acts 7:56

In which verses can the phrase "Son of man" easily be replaced by "I"?

Do these verses express a present time orientation or a future time orientation?

Which verses clearly seem to have a future orientation?

Are there many?

How far into the future does the reference seem to point?

What, then, might you conclude about the future orientation among our ancestors in the faith?

How can you be certain that you have not introduced a middle-class American sense of the future into Mediterranean texts?

Contemporary biblical scholars offer these observations about the phrase "Son of man" and "coming Son of man."

1. The phrase, "Son of man," in early first-century Judaism was not used to describe a supernature or end-of-the-world figure. Thus, it was not an apocalyptic title in Judaism.

2. In the Aramaic language, the one scholars believe that Jesus spoke, the phrase "son of man" is too commonly used to bear the various interpretations which have been placed upon it. Notice in Luke (and the other evangelists) how this "common" phrase often means simply "I."

3. As a result of these insights, scholars deny that Jesus used this phrase of himself in any special way. That "special" use, namely, a "coming Son of man," was more than likely placed on his lips after the resurrection of Jesus on the basis of a rapidly spreading expectation that he would return again very soon, perhaps any week-end.

Scholars believe that this phrase, the "coming Son of man" is the product of Christian scribal interpretation of Daniel 7:13–14 (pause to read and reflect upon it) in the decades following the resurrection of Jesus. The early church, on the basis of its experience with the Risen Jesus, fully expected his imminent return, and with it, the kingdom and the end of the world. The expectation of the imminent end of the world thus originates with the church's expectation of Jesus' return as Son of man.

If you find this discussion different from perceptions and convictions you have previously known and held, keep uppermost in mind the point of this lesson and of this entire book:

> Time is a value that is understood and calculated differently in different cultures.

> Cultural experts note that Mediterranean peasants have no awareness of a future anything like the future middle-class Americans live with.

In the light of these basic insights, how can a middle-class American bible student read the Bible with proper respect for its Mediterranean cultural origins?

Conclusion
In general, the rank-order of value preferences relative to time orientation which characterize the first-century Mediterranean world is:

Present	Past	Future

Remember that every culture offers all three options for time orientation. Diverse groups in the culture, however, arrange or prioritize these options differently according to their special situation and interests. We shall pay more attention to this in the follow-up section.

FOLLOW-UP

It is probably becoming more and more clear by now that the great utility of this model for analyzing and comparing value preferences within a given culture, as well as across cultures, is that it permits an observer to attend to many nuances and peculiarities. The interpreter entrusts much less to an unbridled imagination and instead is encouraged to imagine scenarios more in tune with the culture behind the text than with the interpreter's own cultural situation.

In every culture, there is a prevailing and preferred arrangement of value preferences, and there is also an alternative arrangement preferred by other groups and sometimes even by individual members of those groups.

As noted above, middle-class Americans typically arrange their temporal preferences in this way:

Future	Present	Past

Upper-class Americans, notably those who populate the society pages of the newspapers, display a clear preference for an alternative arrangement:

Past	Present	Future

The rehearsal of one's ancestry and family achievements in these news articles is important for it presents the basis for present status. Ordinarily, accumulated wealth guarantees the future, and hence there is less concern for the future among this class.

At the same time, some American marginal groups, such as the hippies, the beatniks, and the economically deprived are in some ways similar to peasants and evidence the same value preferences as that group, namely:

Present	Future	Past

The present, for people in these groups, is quite engrossing and even burdensome. It leaves room for a modest hope in the future, but no concern for the past.

Do these assessments match the characteristics presented in the chart above?

Would you assess American groups or sub-groups differently?

How would you explain and support your assessment?

The New Testament

The majority of the first-century Palestinian population were peasants, and as noted in this session, the value preferences manifested in their temporal orientation are clearly as follows:

Present	Past	Future

Other groups, like the priests, scribes, and Pharisees

manifest an alternative arrangement of value preferences in their temporal orientation:

Past	Present	Future

READ Luke 1:5–9.

Zechariah, the father of John the Baptizer, was a priest. To which division did he belong (v 5)?

What significance did his membership in this division have? (Read 1 Chronicles 24:1–19.)

What does the 1 Chronicles passage reveal to you?

Is this a warrant from the past for present-time status among priests, descendants of the "sons of Aaron"?

What additional significance, at least in Luke's report, does Zechariah's priestly status have (v 8)?

Do you notice how and why the past is a primary interest among priests rather than the present which is primary among peasants?

READ Luke 3:23–38.

This list of persons is sometimes called a genealogy. It is important to remember that in antiquity, genealogies served a variety of purposes and were often adjusted or re-created to meet new needs.

Does this genealogy seem primarily interested in displaying Jesus' ancestry?

How does the genealogy end (v 38)?

How does this relate to verse 22?

Does it seem that this genealogy is not so much a testimony to Jesus' line of ancestors as it is rather directed back to the previous story (Luke 3:21–22) of Jesus' baptism where he is acclaimed by the voice from heaven: "You are my beloved Son, in you I am well pleased"?

In other words, does this list of ancestors look to the past (as in the case of Zechariah) or does it look more to the present, the event which has just occurred, the baptism of Jesus?

The reader is encouraged to explore Luke's gospel further with the aid of this model of temporal orientations for other indications of diverse value preferences in this regard.

Clearly, any middle-class American interested in reading the New Testament for spiritual benefit or theological reflection recognizes the challenge inherent in the Mediterranean value orientations reflected in biblical texts. As many scholars have pointed out in the past, the Bible is not a "how-to" book. Believers who strive to implement it literally will succeed to the extent that they, too, live in a Mediterranean culture. Believers from other cultures will have to take literally Jesus own instruction given at the end of the story of the Good Samaritan: "Go and do in like manner!" (Not: "Go and do the same thing!" Luke 10:22–37)

Resources

Borg, Marcus J. "A Temperate Case for a Non-Eschatological Jesus," *Forum* 2, 3 (1986), 81–102.

Hall, Edward T. *The Dance of Life: The Other Dimension of Time.* Garden City: Doubleday and Co., 1983.

Levine, Robert, with Ellen Wolff, "Social Time: The Heartbeat of Culture," *Psychology Today*, March, 1985, pp. 29–30.

Malina, Bruce J. "Christ and Time: Swiss or Mediterranean," *Catholic Biblical Quarterly* 51 (1989), 1–31.

UNESCO, *Cultures and Time: At the Cross Roads of Culture.* Paris: UNESCO Press, 1976.

Session Seven

Values and Nature

T he cruise ship *Titanic* was described by its builders as unsinkable. Some researchers have claimed that the captain was fully informed of icebergs in the shipping lanes but was convinced that the ship could run right through them without suffering harm. Through the wisdom of hindsight, everyone now knows that was a serious miscalculation. But on the spot, at that moment, the captain acted upon information that was widely known and accepted. This marvel of human ingenuity was considered to be superior to the forces of nature, stronger than icebergs. In a word, the *Titanic* was unsinkable.

The first-century Mediterranean world took a different view of nature. Shortly after setting sail with seasoned fishermen on the Sea of Galilee, Jesus fell asleep in the boat. A driving storm arose and prompted these fishermen-disciples to wake Jesus by shouting: "We are perishing!" Jesus calmed the storm, and his disciples wondered: "What kind of person is this, that he controls nature, he commands winds and sea, and they obey him?" (Matthew 8:23–27).

Western culture in general holds such a strong faith in human wisdom and technology that it firmly believes nature can and will be mastered. Nature exists to be mastered and controlled. Mediterranean peasants, in contrast, are equally convinced that they are always at the mercy of nature which no human being can master or conquer.

Human perceptions and interpretations of nature, including the human capacity to master it or the need to suffer it, are another major challenge about which cultures differ. In this session, we shall examine and explore the contrasting approaches to nature evident in western culture and Mediterranean culture.

Preparation: The American drive to master nature

Lesson: Mediterranean submission to nature

Follow-up: Further contrasting responses to nature

PREPARATION

Human beings are an integral part of nature. Faced with the power and force of nature, human beings in diverse cultures select one of three possible relationships to nature and arrange them variously in rank-order of preference. Here are the three options.

Mastery over nature—This attitude toward nature is based on the conviction that few if any problems (of any kind) will not yield to technology and the expenditure of huge sums of money. This is a primary value orientation in the west in general and the United States in particular where human sickness, for example, is generally viewed from this perspective. Faith in technology is high. If the human heart fails, an artificial heart created by human beings can replace it. There is no human sickness which human ingenuity and the expenditure of large sums of money cannot conquer, sooner or later.

In addition, advances in modes of transportation have not only made it possible to travel rapidly, as in jet aircraft, but also to travel quite far (to the moon, to distant planets, and even beyond the solar system) with rockets. While some human problems remain, such as war, weather, and some chronic illnesses, hope nevertheless remains high that eventually these, too, can be mastered.

Subjugation or submission to nature—The proverb, "What can't be cured is best endured," aptly describes the attitude of subjugation to nature when nature cannot be mastered. In a culture where nature is routinely mastered, subjugation to nature is a secondary value orientation.

On the other hand, in cultures or cultural subgroups where nature is considered to have power over human life, the attitude of subjection to nature is a primary value orientation. Such an attitude toward nature is especially characteristic of peasants who live in the present, who have no control over their lives, and who feel as if they are at the mercy of forces, personal and impersonal alike. People whose attitude toward nature is subjugation or subjection are most likely to appeal to God for help. If no human being can control or master nature, then God is the only recourse. Obviously, then, in western culture the appeal to God will ordinarily be a second-order value. It generally occurs when human knowledge or intervention fails.

Harmony with nature—This attitude is not very different from the posture of feeling subject to nature. People who live in harmony with nature view human beings as a very integral part of nature, along with gods, demons, angels, saints, spirits, ghosts, leprechauns, and the like. Human misfortune is generally attributed to the fact that a given human being has not paid sufficient attention to keeping life in balance with all these forces. Thus, if it has not rained, the rain god may have been offended. A rain dance might appease the rain god and restore the normal rain pattern, the full harmony of nature!

Cultures differ in the way they arrange their attitudes toward nature. These attitudes, therefore, offer yet another key to understanding scripture. As noted in the story about Jesus and the storm, the first-century Mediterranean fishermen did not have the advantage of long-range weather forecasts, of navigational instruments such as radar or sonar. They felt entirely subjugated to the forces of nature whether these were friendly or hostile. Jesus stands out as a rather exceptional person with his ability to still the storm and to control other dimensions of nature.

Here is the rank-order of value preferences among middle-class Americans regarding nature with an enumeration of some representative characteristics:

MASTERY OVER NATURE	SUBJUGATION TO NATURE	HARMONY WITH NATURE
"technologism"—the universe and the earth exist for human exploitation	"carry one's cross"—the more powerful universe and the earth cannot be controlled; must be suffered	"mind one's place"—the universe and earth function well; negative experiences are the fault of the individual sufferer who must put things aright
"science"—the ability to predict and control nature	"awareness"—the universe and the earth are whimsical, but certainly not predictable	"respect"—the universe and the earth are benign; human beings occasionally fall out of sync
biggest problem = ignorance	biggest problem = powerlessness	biggest problem = violation of rules of nature
ideal solution: prevent or eradicate the problem	ideal solution: alleviate the problem which cannot be eliminated	ideal solution: regain personal integrity in order to restore harmony and balance

The reader is invited to extend this chart, on the basis of further reflection upon mainstream U.S. culture and the Mediterranean culture reflected in the Bible.

Let us now take a closer look at the rank-order of individual middle-class American value preferences regarding nature.

I. Mastery over Nature

In middle-class American culture, the main form of problem-solving for everyday life is self-reliance which is definitely possible once a person masters the technological skills needed to get the job done.

Do you or does someone in your home do the painting, the plumbing, the carpentry, tend to the electrical problems, etc.?

How did this person become adept at these tasks?

What kinds of tools does this person need in order to address problems in any of these areas?

Where are these tools available?

Are they difficult or relatively easy to obtain?

Do you or does someone in your family tend to the lawn and garden?

How does this person deal with insects and other pests?

Have you ever read the list of ingredients in fertilizers or weed- and pest-control chemicals? other lawn or garden applications?

Do you recognize and understand what each ingredient can do?

If not, would it be fair to say you use these various applications "on faith" that they will do the job?

Would you agree that your faith here is primarily in "science" rather than in the "Creator of heaven and earth, and all things living and not living, master of insects, weeds, and the like"?

In the area of personal health care, how do you respond to a burn on your skin in the process of cooking?

Do you put butter or oil on it?

Do you let cold water run over the burn?

Do you apply an ice cube to the burn?

Perhaps you know that the ideal first-aid for a relatively harmless but nonetheless painful skin burn resulting from a cooking accident is the immediate application of something cool, like an ice cube. This is the recommended, appropriate, "scientific" first-aid for a burn.

What would you say to those who still insist on putting butter on a skin burn?

Would you agree that such a person deliberately chooses to remain ignorant?

These are just a few illustrations of the middle-class American conviction that human beings are expected to have almost complete mastery over nature. Someone, somewhere knows the scientific answer or has invented the scientific solution for any problem encountered in nature. The challenge is to learn this solution at some time in life, or to know where to find the appropriate help or solution. Clearly, the biggest problem relative to mastery of nature is ignorance which itself, of course, is easily overcome.

II. Subjugation to Nature

The contemporary experience of AIDS offers an opportunity to analyze the attitude of subjugation or subjection to nature. Here are some statistics, based on incomplete government reporting and therefore probably on the low side, but adequate for discussion purposes. These statistics are drawn from *The New York Times*, Maryland AIDS Administration, and the U.S. Centers for Disease Control:

	Africa	U.S.	MD.	Balto.	D.C.
Pop.	622 mil	246 mil	4.7 mil	753,000	622,000
AIDS since 1981	5 mil	143,286	2,861	1,330	2,448
Deaths since 1981	500,000	87,644	1,742	814	1,531
Cases per 10,000 pop.	80	6	6	17	39

In view of the many diseases which cosmopolitan, scientific medicine has conquered, how do many middle-class Americans view the still unconquered disease of AIDS?

Is there high hope that a cure will be discovered soon?

Do you know anyone who is afflicted with this disease?

Are these people resigned to their fate?

In other words, do middle-class Americans who have AIDS feel powerless before this aspect of nature, but still believe very firmly that very soon medical scientists will learn how to master and control this health problem?

In Uganda, Africa, government officials estimate that a million of the total of 16 million population are infected with the AIDS virus. The Ugandan government and its people are very aware of the problem and also aware of the precautions necessary for avoiding or controlling the disease. Even so, a fatalism reigns among the public. A student at Makerere University reports: "Many of my friends think, 'I probably already have it, or eventually I'll get it anyway, so what's the use of changing.'"

Does this express faith or hope in mastery of nature or rather an inclination toward submitting to nature?

Comparing the cases of death per 10,000 in the chart above, where do you think hope would be high for a cure, and where would you think that hope might be very low?

Do you think residents of Baltimore in particular might be more inclined to pessimism than residents of Maryland in general?

Do these admittedly incomplete figures contribute to false perceptions and interpretations?

How do these perceptions and interpretations reflect the cultural attitudes toward mastery of nature?

Are you familiar with any health-related support groups?

Would you agree that in many cases, members of health-related support groups help each other cope with a problem over which they have little or no control?

In other words, where mastery or control is lacking in middle-class American life, is there a need for assistance in dealing with this deficiency?

The feeling of being subject to nature is a difficult one for most middle-class Americans to imagine. We are so accustomed to being in charge, to mastering our environment, that when our efforts are thwarted or become ineffective, we are totally baffled. Notice how closely the attitude of mastery over nature is linked with another major middle-class American value: "doing." This cluster of middle-class American value preferences (doing, future orientation, individualism, and mastery over nature) make subjection to nature very difficult to imagine and endure.

III. Harmony with Nature

Increased sensitivity to environment and ecology in America has made the attitude of "harmony with nature" more appealing to many middle-class Americans. Still, this orientation toward nature is not a prevailing value except among Native Americans, for whom it is the primary value orientation relative to nature.

Essential to the attitude of "harmony with nature" is the belief that all of nature is good and is intended to exist in perfect balance. Human beings are invariably responsible for disturbing the balance or being unaware of the balance. Thus human beings must make every effort to keep the balance.

Are you familiar with any holistic health programs based on an attitude of harmony with nature?

Do you count any Native Americans among your friends or acquaintances?

Have you ever been encouraged to utilize a Native American remedy?

While teaching a scripture course to native Canadian candidates for ministry, I discovered that I was catching a cold. One student suggested I chew on some "rat root," or drink a tea made of shredded "rat root." This root is so named because it is a favorite among the muskrats who know how to distinguish this health-promoting root from a similar but poisonous root.

I was skeptical, but decided to try a cup of tea. The

remedy seemed to work, though I don't know if it worked any faster or more efficiently than my favorite cold remedies.

When I returned to the medical school in the U.S. where I served on the clinical faculty in the Department of Preventive Medicine, I related this experience to the chairperson. He suggested I send the root to the lab, and he was willing to wager they'd find traces of some drugs or elements already familiar to us which probably were responsible for any relief I or others might feel from the root.

At the same time, he allowed the healing effect might also be the result of "faith." Some physician scientists have pointed out that "all healing is faith healing." If you believe in something, that may definitely help it to be effective. One might interpret this perspective as reflecting the belief that human beings can have mastery or control over nature. Some call this "mind over matter."

What is your opinion?

Can you identify differing orientations toward nature as represented by native Canadians and a scientifically trained western physician?

In summary, middle-class American value orientations toward nature are very obviously headed by absolute confidence in the mastery of nature, particularly by means of technology and the expenditure of huge sums of money. When we turn to the Bible, we shall meet a rather different value orientation.

LESSON

The general, rank-order of value preferences in regard to nature in the first-century Mediterranean world is:

Subjugation to	Harmony with	Mastery over

Notice once again that the *first*-order value preference of middle-class Americans (mastery over nature) is the very last value preference among Mediterranean peasants! American Bible readers are again cautioned to guard against reading their own values and value orientations into these ancient Mediterranean texts. Review the chart above to recall what is entailed in subjugation, subjection, or submission to nature as a primary value orientation. Remember, too, that subjugation to nature blends easily into harmony with nature as a closely related value option. Both stand in stark contrast to mastery over nature.

I. Subjugation to Nature

Because they live at a subsistence level, peasants are very strongly fixed on the present moment. They cannot afford the luxury of dreaming of the future when the present challenge of finding sufficient nourishment, hoping for the continued growth of the planted crop, and similar vital concerns press in with urgency. They are at the mercy of nature.

Against this backdrop, Jesus stands out as one who appears to have mastery over the forces of nature.

READ these summary passages in Matthew:

4:23–24

7:22

8:16

9:35–36

10:1

10:8

11:5

12:27–28

13:54

14:14

14:35–36

15:29–31

21:14

What is recounted in these "summary-style" passages?

In the context of that culture, are these events illustrations of a mastery of nature or a submission to nature?

Who in these accounts is subjugated to nature?

How many different people are identified as having some mastery over these sickness problems?

Is this mastery limited to a few or very widespread and common in the population?

Do these passages highlight the general value orientation of the population toward subjugation to nature?

READ Matthew 6:25–34.

In the last session we looked at Luke's version of this passage (12:22–31) and highlighted the present-time orientation of the passage. Matthew's present-time orientation is evident in verse 34.

Beyond this, can you see any evidence of subjection to nature in this passage?

How do you interpret the "anxiety" verses: 25, 27, 31, 34?

Do these verses express a futility about seeking to master sources of nourishment (eat and drink)?

Do they suggest simply taking life as it happens? (See verse 25.)

Have you as a westerner ever taken this passage seriously?

Do you know of any westerner who has lived according to the advice of this passage?

What is a western believer to do with this obviously Mediterranean-inspired advice?

READ Matthew 13:3–9.

Does this parable reflect the wisdom of having harnessed nature and put it to human use, or does it illustrate a posture of being subject to the vicissitudes of nature: thieving birds, rocky soil, thorns, etc.?

How does the sower in this parable differ from the modern-day farmer or gardener in western civilization?

II. Harmony with Nature

Recall that subjugation to nature often blends into the attitude of living in harmony with nature.

READ Matthew 7:24–27.

What does this passage manifest about the weather (storms)?

How do you interpret the action of the wise man: Does his building practice reflect a mastery over nature or rather an ability gained from experience to live in harmony with it?

How do you interpret the action of the foolish man: Does he not understand the properties of sand?

Does he not know the potential danger from severe weather and strong winds?

Why would a person build on sand?

Do peasants have much choice about the land they might use?

If sand is all one had, what might one do with it?

How might one live in harmony with sandy soil?

READ Matthew 9:16–17.

How would you interpret the examples Jesus uses here?

Is this knowledge about garments and wineskins an example of mastery of these elements or having learned how to live harmoniously with them?

Is the alternative judgment possible?

Does this story highlight how both these orientations (submission to nature and living in harmony with nature) blend into and overlap one another?

III. Mastery over Nature

The healing stories and mighty deeds reported in the gospels clearly indicate mastery over nature. Such mastery is also very extraordinary and unusual in this culture.

READ Matthew 14:22–33.

Notice the fury of the waves in verse 24.

What does Jesus' activity in verse 25 indicate about his abilities relative to nature?

How do you assess Peter's response in verses 29 and 30?

READ Matthew 8:23–27.

What does Jesus do in the midst of this great storm (v 23)?

What do the disciples say to Jesus (v 25)?

What does the disciples' statement reveal about their orientation toward nature: Do they feel in charge, able to master it, or do they feel as if they are at its mercy?

How does Jesus respond to the storm (v 26)?

What attitude toward one who exhibits mastery over nature does the final comment of the disciples reveal (v 27)?

This kind of mastery over nature belonged to some but certainly not to many members of this culture.

READ Matthew 12:22–45.

Who is brought to Jesus (v 22)?

How does Jesus help this man (v 22)?

In the subsequent comments (vv 24–28), can more than one person cast out demons?

Read verses 43–45 to complete Jesus' comments on exorcism.

Scholars point out that in the New Testament, Jesus generally has no access to power at all, ever, *except* when dealing with evil spirits and demons.

READ these possession stories.

Matthew 8:28–34

9:32–34

12:22–24

15:21–28

17:14–18

In the Mediterranean world, power is a value that belongs to the realm of politics. Thus Jesus' clear exercise of power over demons (and illness) would be perceived by citizens of that culture as political actions. People with power had to have a legitimate claim to it.

READ Matthew 21:23–27.

Who comes to investigate Jesus' authority (v 23)?

Do these people possess a legitimate claim to power?

Isn't it quite natural for them to be concerned about someone not of their group who appears to wield power?

What exact question do they ask of Jesus (v 23)?

What does Jesus answer (vv 24–25)?

Power is wielded in the attempt to explain, predict, and control reality. The power that is exercised in ancient (and contemporary) healing activity definitely attempts to explain (diagnose), predict (prognose) and control (apply the therapy to) the reality known as sickness. Here is one illustration of Jesus' use of power.

RETURN TO Matthew 12:22–45.

How did Jesus and those around him "diagnose" the sick person brought to him (v 22)?

The text doesn't tell us the process they used, but there seemed to be no disagreement about how this person was identified: "a blind and dumb demoniac."

What therapy did Jesus apply (vv 22, 28)?

In a later reflection, what does Jesus prognosticate (vv 43–44)?

Is this not equivalent to pointing out that this healed man's condition can deteriorate?

What, then, is Jesus' final "therapeutic" advice on the subject (v 30)?

The one who acknowledges Jesus' ability to diagnose, to make a prognosis, and to apply therapy need have no worries. In other words, the one who acknowledges Jesus' power and pledges personal loyalty to him (this is what "faith" means) will be well taken care of.

There is no doubt Jesus was successful in this use of power regarding exorcisms and healings.

In the light of this explanation of Jesus' healings and exorcisms, recall again the concern of the chief priests and elders (Matthew 21:23–27), then

READ Matthew 26:3–5.

What have the chief priests and elders of the people decided to do about Jesus' use of power?

Would you agree, then, that Jesus' mighty deeds could be viewed in his culture as political acts?

If these are unauthorized political acts, what judgment do the authorities make?

The very value that middle-class Americans cherish and cultivate (mastery over nature) had some devastating effects in the Mediterranean world. What a difference in cultures!

FOLLOW-UP

Attitudes toward nature are one more basic human challenge in regard to which cultures select differing responses. The stance of middle-class Americans in general toward nature is:

Mastery over	Subjugation to	Harmony with

Our Mediterranean ancestors in the faith organize their value orientations toward nature in this way:

Subjugation to	Harmony with	Mastery over

Another reflection topic which can help a modern, western, Bible reader to appreciate this difference in value orientations is pain and suffering.

READ Matthew 16:21–28.

This passage is the first in a series of three passion predictions in Matthew's gospel.

What does Jesus say about his destiny (v 21)?

How does Peter respond (v 22)?

What is Jesus' retort (v 23)?

As Jesus continues, he presents a challenge to anyone who would be his follower (v 24).

As a mainstream, U.S., believer committed to mastery of nature and mastery of life and one's life situation, how would you interpret this challenge of Jesus?

How does this very sensible Mediterranean advice reflecting submission to events square with the common American conviction of being in charge of events?

READ Matthew 17:22–23.

What does Jesus say?

Does he give any hint of being able to master the situation, or is the attitude rather one of submitting to the situation?

How do the disciples respond (v 23)?

READ Matthew 20:17–19.

What does Jesus say?

Do the disciples make any response?

Or does life go on as usual (vv 20–28)?

Notice verses 22 and 23. Do they suggest mastery over life or submission to life?

In the light of the Mediterranean value preferences regarding nature which we have examined in this session, do these passion prediction passages stand out as something unusual or rather something quite in accord with the culture's values?

READ Matthew 26:36–46.

What is reported in this passage?

What is Jesus' attitude in the face of imminent death (v 38)?

What is Jesus' prayer (v 39)?

If a middle-class American youngster realized that his parent had a particularly difficult fate in mind for the future, would that youngster voice a similar prayer?

Do we not rather wonder why abused children or spouses simply do not flee the situation?

How do you reflect on these and similar situations in the light of the value differences we have been examining relative to mainstream U.S. and Mediterranean cultures?

Conclusion

The contrasting attitudes toward nature (master it; suffer it) which we have examined in this chapter seem to come into sharp focus in the discussion of human pain and suffering.

Cultures which have the ability and means to master pain and suffering view them as a nuisance. Such cultures experience great difficulty appreciating the value of a concept such as "redemptive suffering." Driven by the conviction that nature exists to be mastered by human beings, members of such cultures expend energy and resources to wipe out all suffering. Only such a culture can advertise medicine with the phrase: "When you haven't got time for the pain . . . use x-product!"

Other cultures, like the ones reflected in the pages of the Bible, are convinced that only God has power over nature. Human beings are a part of nature and are subject to it. Jesus' refusal to accept the analgesic drink offered to him on the cross stands in contrast to mainstream U.S. citizens who seek alleviation for pain.

Neither culture is wrong. Members of each of these cultures live according to their respective and respected cultural beliefs. It is therefore possible to develop at least two different "spiritualities" on the basis of these contrasting cultural preferences.

In our final session, we shall examine one more set of contrasting values and then propose one possible, biblically inspired, American, "spiritual" response.

Resources

Pilch, John J. "Reading Matthew Anthropologically: Healing in Cultural Perspective," *Listening: Journal of Religion and Culture* 24 (1989), 278–289.

Pilch, John J. "The Health Care System in Matthew: A Social Science Analysis," *Biblical Theology Bulletin* 16 (1986), 102–106.

Pilch, John J. "Interpreting Scripture: The Social Science Method—A Look at Pain and Leprosy," *The Bible Today,* January, 1988, 13–19.

Spiegel, John. "An Ecological Model of Ethnic Families," pp. 31–51 in Monica McGoldrick, John K. Pearce, and Joseph Giordano, eds., *Ethnicity and Family Therapy.* New York/London: The Guilford Press, 1981.

White, Leland J. "Peacemakers in Matthew's World," *The Bible Today,* January, 1985, 30–35.

Session Eight

Values and Human Nature

"*I*'m O.K.; you're O.K.*"*

Remember this book? It popularized and simplified transactional analysis, a process for improving human relationships. The foundation of this process is the conviction that all people are *basically good* or *neutral* and capable of improving themselves no matter what their situation.

This book could only succeed in modern-day America because it precisely reflects the prevalent mainstream, U.S. cultural conviction about human nature. Contemporary Americans believe that human beings are basically neutral, most likely good, and definitely perfectible. Human growth and development programs thrive not only in California but in many states all across the country. Wisconsin is known as the Wellness Capital of the United States, and many New England and Middle Atlantic states are home base for holistic health centers.

The Mediterranean world takes a different view of human nature. Paul gives a very clear expression to the Mediterranean cultural conviction that human nature is a *mixture of good and evil.*

But I tell you to walk by the Spirit, and do not seek to please the flesh. One who pleases the flesh engages in immorality, impurity, licentiousness, idolatry, envy, dissension, selfishness, anger, idolatry, enmity, sorcery, divisiveness, drunkenness, envy, carousing, and much more. But one who follows the Spirit is marked by love, peace, goodness, fidelity, gentleness, patience, self-control, kindness, and similar virtues. (Galatians 5:16–22 paraphrased)

Rather than "I'm O.K.; you're O.K.," it might be more appropriate to describe Paul's position as "I might not be O.K.; and you might not be O.K."

Assessing and interpreting human nature is another fundamental challenge faced by cultures. Each culture determines a specific interpretation of human nature which serves as its basic value orientation in this regard. Cultures can change their interpretations over time. The initial Puritan outlook on human nature has been replaced by a much more favorable one in the United States. In this session, as in the previous sessions of this program, we are interested in comparing contemporary mainstream U.S. culture with ancient Mediterranean culture.

Preparation: American view: human nature is neutral

Lesson: Mediterranean view: human nature is mixed

Follow-up: The complete model for comparing values across cultures

PREPARATION

It is possible to make one of three assessments of human nature. These three assessments are the options from which cultures choose and order their choices in rank preference.

Human nature is essentially good—This perspective does not see any evil in human nature. Of course, there are evil people, but these are such because evil exceeds the good in them. In this case, evil might originate in the environment but it most certainly does not come from within the person.

In this view, human beings can be trusted to turn out well because their instincts are essentially good. At the same time, good people are capable of being corrupted. One must always be on guard against potential threats to basic goodness.

In the United States, this "good but corruptible" view of human nature found expression in the 1960s among the "flower children" who fled the wicked cities to take refuge in rural settings where basically good human beings could be developed into good citizens, far removed from the pernicious influences of wicked civilization. The roots of this perspective reach back to Rousseau's reflections upon field reports by early South Sea voyagers describing the noble savages they had discovered. How soon these noble savages were corrupted by civilization!

Human nature is essentially evil—In United States culture, this view has always been popular, though its supporters have differed in the course of time. Christian fundamentalists have always promoted it. In recent times, born-again Christians have resurrected the position. In times of national stress, the citizenry at large or sizable segments of the population tend to perceive an alarming element of evil in the culture. For instance, during the stressful recovery from World War II, many Americans were convinced that Communists had infiltrated the government, the motion picture industry, and other media. Communists used to be judged as basically evil. Recall President Reagan's embarrassing epithet of the Soviet Union: "The Evil Empire."

Human nature is essentially mixed—That is, a mixture of good and evil. This orientation believes that human nature contains the potential for both good and evil because it contains both tendencies. In the Hebrew tradition, there is a belief in "two tendencies" which are innate in the human person. These tendencies are called the *yeṣer hatob* (the good tendency) and the *yeṣer hara* (the evil tendency). This belief existed in Judaism at the time of Christ, is reflected in the New Testament (see Galatians 5:16–22), and has endured in the rabbinic tradition as well.

> For the grain of evil seed (the *yeṣer hara*) was sown in Adam's heart from the beginning, and how much ungodliness it has produced until now, and will produce until the time of threshing comes! (4 Ezra 4:30)

Human nature is essentially neutral—There is yet a fourth possible perspective on human nature that scholars recognize, but it appears to be distinctive to contemporary United States culture. Initially, the Puritan settlers in America believed and taught that people were born evil but were perfectible. Evil people could be perfected by repentance stirred by sermons such as the classic "Sinners in the hands of an angry God." Religiously oriented colleges and divinity schools also contributed toward perfecting evil people.

But with the advent of nineteenth-century humanism, an increase of secular colleges and universities, and the popularization of psychology and the social sciences in the twentieth century, belief in the original sinfulness of human nature was displaced by acceptance of a neutral orientation. In this view, human beings are born neither good nor evil but rather "neutral" and thus are susceptible to the influences of the environment, parents and guardians, the neighborhood, and the educational system. This neutral position also does away with divine punishment for sins. Instead, it generates a moral pragmatism. Although there is a general belief that we should not inflict harm on others, only specific laws and a personal sense of decency guarantee that this kindness will indeed be put into practice.

Experts indicate that the rank-order of value preferences among middle-class Americans relative to human nature is as follows:

Neutral	Evil	Good

Take some time to reflect upon the attitudes toward human nature expressed in this rank-ordering of value preferences.

I. Human Nature is Neutral

The attitude that human nature is neutral in nature just waiting to be properly shaped, molded, guided, can be highlighted in a variety of human behaviors. It is considered a key element in American core culture.

Luke reports that when Jesus was born, Mary "wrapped him in swaddling cloths" and laid him in a manger (Luke 2:7).

Why are children wrapped in swaddling cloths?

Were you wrapped in swaddling cloths as a child?

Were your own children or children in your family wrapped in swaddling cloths?

There are many reasons why infants are wrapped in swaddling cloths. Specialists in Mediterranean culture observe that the purpose of swaddling infants is to accustom them as soon as possible to restriction, rigidity, inflexibility, submission, obedience, and a host of similar values. Swaddling cloths restrict infant mobility. The infant must learn obedience and submission to others.

How are middle-class American youngsters laid in their cribs?

Are they wrapped tightly in swaddling cloths?

Or are they generally just diapered and left relatively free to wave their arms and legs?

This is one middle-class American behavior pattern that highlights the conviction that human nature is "neutral." It is not to be feared, it does not have to be reined in as early as possible. Human beings can and should be encouraged to develop in freedom, complete freedom from restraint, which is another core value of American culture.

II. Human Nature is Evil

In American culture, this perspective on human nature is the contemporary second-order possibility, but it is always considered a possibility.

Christian fundamentalists and others who speak of an "original sinfulness" of human beings typify one attitude that represents a belief that human nature is evil.

Have any door-to-door evangelists ever stopped by to tell you that you are in need of salvation, of being born-again, of being reborn, of needing repentance, or the like?

How did you respond?

How was your response received?

How did you ultimately settle the discussion?

Do you think human nature or human beings are basically and fundamentally evil, or inclined toward evil?

The 1990 "Crisis in the Gulf" involving Iraq, Kuwait, and the United States as well as other nations of the world community offered a fresh opportunity for analyzing the effect of "national stress" upon American outlooks on human nature.

Generally speaking, Americans believe human nature is "neutral" and capable of being developed along good lines.

Can you recall any of the adjectives used by leaders and repeated in the media to describe Saddam Hussein, the President of Iraq?

Was he called "butcher"? "crazy"? "insane"? "madman"?

Can you recall other adjectives?

Was Saddam Hussein viewed as basically neutral but excessively inclined to evil?

Or does it rather seem that this period of national stress in the United States caused many to assess another human being as having a basically "evil" nature?

Can you think of other examples in recent American history where similar outlooks were reflected regarding leaders of other countries with whom the United States had fallen out of favor?

Does this seem to you to illustrate how periods of national stress change the prevailing American cultural view of human nature?

Does this help you to appreciate why cultural experts list the conviction that "human nature is evil" as a second-order value preference of mainstream U.S. culture?

III. Human Nature is Good

It is no doubt surprising to many readers to learn that a view of human nature as good is a *last-order* value preference among contemporary, middle-class Americans. Indeed, to be exact, the complete concept is: "good but corruptible." Expert analysts of American culture are quite in agreement on this point as well.

It seems possible to describe the outlooks of Dr. James Dobson, the well-known authority on discipline, as representative of this outlook:

> It would be grossly unfair to say that most young people are "bad"; they are merely responding to social forces and causes that are leading them into the face of disaster. (*Dare to Discipline.* Wheaton: Tyndale House, 1970, p. 19)

It is also possible to view the distrustful parenting orientation toward children (see *Hear the Word!* Book One, Session Four), one that relies on physical punishment—as Dr. Dobson recommends—as a reflection of this same orientation toward human nature.

As often as I have presented the contrasting approaches to disciplining youngsters (trustful versus distrustful; calm reasoning versus physical spanking), those who favor spanking and physical punishment remind me that they do this with love, because they love the youngsters.

Few would doubt that such people sincerely love their children and sincerely believe that physical discipline is an expression of love.

Whatever the motive, physical punishment nevertheless seems to represent the view that human nature is indeed good but corruptible. Physical punishment is a kind of preventive medicine to ensure that a given human nature continues to strive to be good.

Another child-rearing or parenting strategy that can be associated with this outlook is that described as "tough love." Advocates of this strategy do not believe the youngsters are evil. They have merely gone temporarily astray or are misguided. Serious discipline administered as a form of "tough love" should bring deviant children back to their senses unless they have become totally and hopelessly corrupt.

Summary

Remember that the purpose of a model is to facilitate understanding. The model for analyzing values across cultures which we are examining in this book is intended to help readers grasp and appreciate cultural differences relative to fundamental human values. Certainly human nature is cherished as an important "given" of existence. Attitudes toward human nature, however, vary across cultures. Experts in the study and analysis of culture note that in contemporary, middle-class American culture, human nature is assessed in this rank-order: human nature is neutral, is evil, is good-but-corruptible. As we shall notice in the next section, our Mediterranean ancestors in the faith took a slightly different view of human nature.

LESSON

The general rank-order of value preferences relative to human nature in the first-century Mediterranean world is:

Mixed	Evil	Good

This rank-order reflects the preferences of Jewish peasants, the Pharisees, and Jesus.

Notice that the American preference, "Neutral," is missing from this arrangement. The American position in this regard is distinctive in world cultures and is not applicable to the Mediterranean cultural context.

I. Human Nature is Mixed

The perspective that views human nature as a mixture of good and evil tendencies is very common in many cultures. In the Mediterranean world, it has varied expressions. The Jewish belief in these two tendencies in rooted in Genesis 2:7.

READ Genesis 2:7.

The Hebrew word for "formed" is *ysr*, and in this verse it has two "y's." Ancient interpreters of the Hebrew Bible deduced from this fact that God had created in this first human being two impulses: one good, and one bad.

Further evidence for the evil tendency was found in two additional verses:

READ Genesis 6:5–8.

How does God assess "imagination of the thoughts of a human being's heart"?

How serious is the evil located there?

What does God intend to do about this (v 7)?

Does God make an exception (v 8)?

READ Genesis 8:20–22.

What did Noah do after the flood (v 20)?

How did God respond to what Noah did (v 21)?

What did God promise (v 21)?

What is God's judgment here about human beings (v 21)?

Has God's judgment changed since Genesis 6:5?

It is important to note that these are impulses in nature. They are not intrinsically evil, but they lead to evil consequences when the human being yields to the impulse and consciously commits unlawful deeds. Belief in these two impulses is interpreted as a belief that human nature is a mixture of good and evil tendencies. This Jewish belief was certainly alive in the first century and is reflected in different parts of the New Testament.

READ Mark 7:1–23.

Recall what was said in session one, above, about the first sixteen verses of this chapter in Mark's gospel.

What is the topic about which Jesus and his enemies are in conflict? (See verses 2, 5, and 14.)

What is Jesus' opinion about things that "defile" (vv 18 to 23)?

Would you agree that Jesus here has clearly accepted and commented upon the Jewish belief in the "evil tendency" in human nature as explained in the preceding texts from Genesis?

READ Galatians 5:16–26.

When Paul contrasts the terms "Spirit" and "flesh" some

scholars believe that his use of the term "flesh" echoes his belief in the "evil tendency" which exists in human nature alongside the "good tendency."

How does Paul contrast these two terms (vv 16–18)?

What does the "flesh" or the "evil tendency" lead to (vv 19–21)?

What does the "Spirit" or the "good tendency" lead to (vv 22–23)?

What does Paul expect the good Christian to do (vv 24–26)?

Did you notice the "communal" orientation of Paul in the final verse (26)?

Does this perspective make a difference in how one might read the contrasts?

II. Human Nature is Evil

The secondary value preference in Mediterranean culture seems most strongly reflected in Paul's assessment of human nature.

READ Romans 5:12–21.

These verses have stimulated intense debate and caused deep divisions among Christians over the centuries. The Council of Trent (1545) declared that in these verses Paul does appear to teach some form of an original failure or sin. But one must also note that neither Paul nor Trent used this exact phrase: "original sin."

When did "sin" originate (vv 12 and 13)?

It is important to realize that Paul understands "sin" to be a force or a power, active within and among all human beings. When he uses this word, he is not automatically talking about *specific and individual sins*. Most of the time he refers to "sin" as a "force" in human experience.

Would you see in Romans 5 a suggestion that human nature is tainted, or evil, since the failure of the first creature?

How was the situation remedied (vv 15–19)?

What is Paul's exhortation in Romans 6:12–14?

READ Romans 7:14–20.

Some scholars believe that this passage echoes Paul's affirmation of the common Jewish belief at the time in the "two innate tendencies" in human nature: toward good and toward evil.

What presumably common, human awareness does Paul express (vv 15, 19, 22)?

Would you agree that Paul is voicing his experience of the struggle between two tendencies in human nature?

What is Paul's desperate prayer (vv 24–25)?

Who indeed can deliver Paul and others from this struggle? (READ Romans 8:9–14.)

Still other scholars think that deep down, Paul believes human nature is basically evil, that it was rendered such by the failure of the first creature, Adam, whose failure was affirmed by his descendants in their own failures.

READ 1 Corinthians 10:1–13.

Did all the Israelites experience God's protection (vv 1–4)?

How did God judge them? all? some? most? (v 5)

What was disturbing about their behavior (vv 6–10)?

Notice Paul's opinion about what has prompted this displeasing behavior (vv 11–13).

Where do these temptations come from (v 13)?

Is there any hope to withstand these struggles?

Another passage that might be interpreted as reflecting Paul's conviction that human nature is basically evil is found in Galatians.

READ Galatians 4:8–10.

Notice the condition of the Galatians "before" they came to know God (v 8).

Does this suggest an evaluation of human nature as basically evil?

What happened next?

Is a relapse possible (v 11)?

Even among the disciples of Paul who wrote letters in his name, this attitude toward human nature seems to remain. The author of 1 and 2 Timothy and Titus is considered to be a disciple of Paul and is often called "The Pastor."

READ 1 Timothy 1:12–17.

How does "The Pastor" describe the earlier period of his life (v 13)?

What changed things (v 14)?

Who did Jesus come to save (v 15)?

Is it reasonable to take this as confirmation of a belief that human nature is basically evil, sinful, in need of repair?

READ Titus 3:1–8.

What does "The Pastor" exhort Titus to do (v 1)?

How does "The Pastor" describe an earlier period of his life (v 3)?

What changed things (vv 4–7)?

Is this assessment of human nature and its improvement a strong conviction with "The Pastor" (v 8)?

In summary, these select passages do seem to reveal a belief that human nature is basically flawed, rendered so by the fall of Adam and its subsequent validation by the personal failures of all his descendants. In the Christian perspective, this comes to light especially in the redemption offered by Jesus.

III. Human Nature is Good

This last-order value preference in the Mediterranean perspective on human nature is obviously rooted in Genesis.

READ Genesis 1:1–2:3.

What is God's assessment of each moment of creation? (See for instance, 1:4.)

How many times in this narrative does God make this assessment?

In the rabbinic tradition, this scripture narrative produced a very interesting judgment on the "two tendencies" in human nature.

Rabbi Samuel ben Naḥman in Genesis Rabbah 9,7 offers this comment on Genesis 1:31 (God saw that everything he made was very good):

> "And behold it was very good." This is the "evil tendency." Is then the evil tendency good? Yet were it not for the evil tendency no man would build a house, nor marry a wife, nor beget children, nor engage in trade. Solomon said "All labor and all excelling in work is a man's rivalry with his neighbor." (Qoheleth 4:4)

The rabbinic tradition concluded that all human appetites and passions are such an essential part of human nature, and so necessary to the preservation of life and the continuity of civilization, that they should not be eradicated or suppressed but most certainly controlled and directed.

There appear to be in the gospels at least some traces of an attitude that human nature is good, at least sometimes.

READ Mark 9:38–40.

Why did Jesus' disciples forbid an exorcist to cast out demons in Jesus' name (v 38)?

In the light of what you recall about Jesus forming a special group about himself (see *Hear the Word!* Session One commenting on Mark 7), wouldn't it make sense for the disciples to be discriminating about group membership? Shouldn't they be careful about just who is "in" and who is "out" of their group?

What did Jesus respond (v 39)?

Does Jesus' comment hint that perhaps the disciples stumbled upon a man of decency, an upright man?

Look closer at Jesus' comment. Does it seem to have a "before" and "after" dimension?

Can you identify the "before" and "after"?

Would you say this is similar to the "before" and "after" evident in Paul and "The Pastor"? (Before, we were sinners; after redemption, we are good.)

What conclusion would you draw about Jesus' view in this passage then?

On the other hand, there is at least one clear passage that indicates Mediterranean culture did not view human nature as good. Indeed, this view is, as indicated, a third-order value preference in first-century Mediterranean culture.

READ Mark 10:17–22.

How does the petitioner in verse 17 address Jesus?

How does Jesus answer (v 18)?

How would you relate Jesus' answer here with the sentiment expressed in the incident above (Mark 9:38–40)?

Doesn't this sound like Jesus is denying that human nature is basically good?

Can you think of another interpretation?

The "Evil Eye"

Recall the discussion of the pervasive Mediterranean belief in the "evil eye" in session two of this book. The "evil eye" is a synonym for envy accompanied by a wish to damage the person or thing envied. In Mediterranean cultures, compliments are always suspect as insincere, as a cover for envy, and as disguising a wish that the thing envied would be destroyed or diminished.

Even if the compliment seems to be a truly honest and uncontrolled expression of sentiment, the Mediterranean cultural belief is convinced that capricious and malevolent spirits who permeate the air around human beings and who hear this compliment will be tempted to do damage or behave mischievously toward the one complimented. They might do something to lessen the "good" that was admired.

Generally, a verbal compliment will be very carefully phrased and most often accompanied by hand gestures or other body language to signal sincerity and to assure the listener that no evil is intended.

In this story, while Jesus' rejection of the adjective "good" might be interpreted as reflecting his culture's primary value orientation relative to human nature (it is a mixture of good and evil), it is also possible to interpret his rejection as a deliberate attempt to ward off any potential evil that the spirits might inflict upon him on account of this compliment.

READ Mark 1:9–13.

Who is present at Jesus' baptism (vv 9 *and* 5!)?

In addition to all these people, do you think the air around these people was crowded with spirits of all kinds (from a Mediterranean cultural perspective)?

What descended upon Jesus (v 10)?

Was a compliment paid to Jesus (v 11)?

Who paid this compliment?

Who heard this compliment?

What happened after the compliment was paid (vv 12–13)?

In the context of the Mediterranean belief in the "evil eye" understood as damage-threatening envy, do you think that perhaps the reason why the story of the temptation of Jesus follows immediately after his baptism is because of the "envy" stirred by the compliment about him? Would this be the Mediterranean cultural interpretation of his temptation, that envious spirits were trying to undo his "good reputation" proclaimed by God?

Like all written texts, so too the scripture frequently omits body language and gestures that accompany speech. It is quite possible that the compliment directed to Jesus in Mark 10:17 sparked in Jesus a common, cultural fear of "the evil eye," jealousy, potentially damaging envy. Besides uttering an explicit denial of the compliment and giving a reason for the denial ("No one is good but God alone"), it is also possible that Jesus spit. (See Galatians 4:14 where Paul, whom the Galatians suspect of having an evil eye, says: "though my condition was a trial to you, you did not spit at or despise me.") Spitting was and is a commonly used gesture to protect against the evil eye or evil spirits. Jesus might also have used a hand gesture to ward off the compliment: hand extended with palm facing outward and fingers upward. Both of these body-language strategies normally accompany verbal protestations in Mediterranean cultural experiences where the evil eye is suspected to be operative.

FOLLOW-UP

Assessments of human nature are yet another basic human challenge on which cultures differ. The stance of middle-class Americans, rather unique on the planet, is that human nature is

Neutral	Evil	Good

in this precise rank-order. As noted above, Americans arrived at this neutral position after abandoning the early Puritan conviction that human nature is fundamentally evil but redeemable.

The Mediterranean peasant perspective is that human nature is rather:

Mixed	Evil	Good

This session offers some examples from each culture and invites the readers to identify additional examples from their own cultural experiences as well as their in-depth Bible study.

As a follow-up to this session and a general conclusion to the preceding four sessions, here are two charts to assist readers in their further reflections on these topics.

I. A Model for Comparing Values across Cultures

Each session from four through eight focused on a specific element of a larger model for comparing values across cultures. Here is that complete model in full.

PROBLEM 1: Selecting a principal mode of HUMAN ACTIVITY

RANGE OF SOLUTIONS:

Being   Being-in-becoming   Doing

PROBLEM 2: RELATIONSHIPS of human beings TO EACH OTHER

RANGE OF SOLUTIONS:

Collateral   Lineal   Individual

PROBLEM 3: Determining the primary TEMPORAL FOCUS OF LIFE

RANGE OF SOLUTIONS:

Present   Past   Future

PROBLEM 4: RELATIONSHIPS of human beings TO NATURE

RANGE OF SOLUTIONS:

Be subject to it   Live in harmony with it   Master it

PROBLEM 5: Prevailing ASSESSMENT OF HUMAN NATURE

RANGE OF SOLUTIONS:

Mixture of good   Evil   Good
and evil

Chart taken from John J. Pilch, "Marian Devotion and Wellness Spirituality: Bridging Cultures," *Biblical Theology Bulletin* 20 (1990), 85–94.

First notice the five common problems faced by each culture. Each of the last five sessions has focused on one of these problems or challenges.

Second, each culture has a limited range of solutions for each problem. Actually there are only three. Relative to the assessment of human nature, we noticed that middle-class American culture and Mediterranean culture each have solutions, but one of these three is different in each culture. Americans believe human nature to be neutral, but the Mediterranean and all other cultures of the world believe human nature to be a mixture of good and evil.

Third, while each culture selects one of the three solutions as primary, the other two are also available as second and third choice solutions either for different circumstances or for different sub-groups in one and the same culture. We have pointed out these varied arrangements in Mediterranean culture much more than in American culture. American readers should have little difficulty exploring other arrangements available in their native culture. To assist such exploration, the following section offers another useful chart.

II. Sketch of Value Orientation Profiles Explored in This Book

VALUE ORIENTATION PROFILES

	Italian Rural			Roman			Greek		
Activity	Be	> BiB	> Do	BiB	> Be	> Do	Be	> Do	> BiB
Relational	Coll	> Lin	> Ind	Lin	> Coll	> Ind	Lin	> Ind	> Coll
Time	Pres	> Past	> Fut	Past	> Pres	> Fut	Pres	> Past	> Fut
Man-Nature	Sub	> With	> Over	Over	> With	> Sub	Sub	> With	> Over
Human nature	Mixed	> Evil	> Good	Good	> Mixed	> Evil	Mixed	> Evil	> Good

	Israelite Peasant			Judean Elite			Pharisees		
Activity	Be	> BiB	> Do	Be	> Bib	> Do	Be	> Do	> BiB
Relational	Coll	> Lin	> Ind	Lin	> Coll	> Ind	Lin	> Ind	> Coll
Time	Pres	> Past	> Fut	Pres	> Past	> Fut	Past	> Pres	> Fut
Man-Nature	Sub	> With	> Over	Over	> With	> Sub	Sub	> With	> Over
Human nature	Mixed	> Evil	> Good	Mixed	> Evil	> Good	Mixed	> Evil	> Good

	Jesus			Paul			American		
Activity	Bib	> Be	> Do	Bib	> Be	> Do	Do	> Be	> BiB
Relational	Coll	> Ind	> Lin	Lin	> Coll	> Ind	Ind	> Coll	> Lin
Time	Pres	> Past	> Fut	Pres	> Past	> Fut	Fut	> Pres	> Past
Man-Nature	With	> Sub	> Over	Sub	> With	> Over	Over	> Sub	> With
Human nature	Mixed	> Evil	> Good	Evil	> Mixed	> Good	Neutral	> Evil	> Good

Chart from John J. Pilch and Bruce J. Malina, eds., *Dictionary of New Testament Values*. Peabody, MA.: Hendrickson Press, 1991.

Notice how well the primary or dominant value choices fit together in each culture.

Middle-class American culture favors *Doing* which places strong emphasis upon personal achievement. Achievement is facilitated by being able to plan for the *future,* which in its turn is made easier by the culture's emphasis on the *individual* unhampered by family or group ties. Moreover, the optimism generated by the cultural conviction of the human ability to have *mastery over nature* is further strengthened by the pragmatic morality which derives from taking a basically *neutral view of human nature.*

Can you identify the pressure points in this complex of primary value orientations?

For instance, can an emphasis on achievement lead to workaholism?

If mastery of nature is a central conviction, how does one handle tragedy?

Is tragedy just chalked up to human error or stupidity?

What other stress point can you identify?

Scholars point to yet another curious feature about the rank-order of value preferences this model helps to generate for any given culture. Relative to middle-class

American culture, the primary value orientations presented above generally apply principally to *men*! Until very
recent times, women have generally been socialized into
the second-order alternative values.

Thus, American women have generally been expected to attend to everyday matters (*Present*). This culture
has also expected them to demonstrate emotion and look
after the emotional needs of spouse and children (*Being*).
It has also generally been their lot to be sensitive to relatives and friends, for instance, keeping track of birthdays,
anniversaries, special observances, cultivating family
social events, etc. (*Collateral or group focus*).

Can you fill in the remaining two value orientations
for middle-class American women?

If you are an American-ethnic, you will very likely be
able to chart still other configurations.

Mediterranean Culture as Reflected in the New Testament

The constant reminders of Jesus to "do" the will of God as
well as the Old Testament reminders to "observe" the commandments were a necessary stimulus for a culture whose
primary value orientation was to *Being* rather than Doing.

The constant interplay between Sadducees, Pharisees, scribes, Jesus' disciples, and others clearly reflects
the culture's preference for *group focus* or *collateral relationships*. Moreover, the fact that so few people in the
gospels have names (a woman with a flow of blood, a
man with a withered hand, a paralytic, etc.) reflects low
interest in individualism accompanied by a tendency to
stereotype others: for instance, "Jews have no dealings
with Samaritans" (John 4:9).

A quite natural and appropriate accompaniment to an orientation to spontaneous response to experiences (*Being*) is the culture's focus on the *Present*: "Give us *today* our daily bread!"

Moreover, a culture that is not dedicated to *Doing* and achieving but is interested only in the *Present* rather than the future is not likely to find an interest in mastery over nature, but will be resigned to *living in submission to nature*.

The belief that human nature is a *mixture of good and evil* only contributes to the unwillingness to take a risk in *Doing* and a preference for simply responding to situations as they occur (*Being*).

As in all cultures, women in the Mediterranean world are usually socialized into the second-order preferences as *their* primary value orientation. Thus, Mediterranean women are and were routinely considered as possessing an evil human nature. "From a woman sin had its beginning, and because of her we all die" (Sirach 25:24). If men are primarily oriented to Being, spontaneously enjoying the Present moment and its challenge, women are primarily oriented toward Doing and a concern for passing on Past traditions to the present crop of youngsters. When Jesus healed her, Peter's mother-in-law did not run about and spread the word (*Being*! as healed men did), but instead "served them" (*Doing*! Mark 1:29–31).

Flesh out the complete picture for women with additional examples. Remember not to force any evidence into the model. The model is flexible and serves only as a tool for highlighting evidence that might otherwise escape the most attentive, but highly ethnocentric, eyes.

Conclusion

A large part of this book has been devoted to an in-depth examination of a model for comparing values across cultures. This model is also useful for constructing an American theology or spirituality that respects but does not distort or misinterpret its biblical inspiration.

Wellness spirituality is one such attempt to respect and seriously consider the primary value orientations of American culture as a reliable foundation for a spiritual life. Because the Mediterranean primary value orientations that characterize the Bible are secondary and tertiary value orientations in the American scheme, a person who would integrate the two will seek to find a balance. It would be erroneous to totally discard one's own cultural values only to replace them with the values of an alien culture.

Wellness spirituality celebrates "doing" but also encourages "being." It suggests that individualism works well when balanced by appropriate collateral relationships. To ward off potentially excessive focus on the future, it urges the American to pay more attention to the present. Mastery over nature needs to be tempered with a healthy respect for limits and with an attempt to live in respectful harmony with nature. And while Americans do not view human nature as evil, honesty requires the admission that it is not entirely neutral, either.

The United States bishops exhort believers to "place the Sacred Scriptures at the heart of parish and individual life." The cross-cultural approach to interpreting scripture promoted in *Hear the Word!* makes a modest contribution to making the bishops' wish a reality for believers in United States parishes.

Resources

Arensberg, Conrad and Arthur H. Niehoff. "American Cultural Values," pp. 363–378 in C. Arensberg and A. Niehoff, eds., *Introducing Social Change.* Chicago: Aldine-Atherton, Inc., 1971.

Gilmore, David D., ed. *Honor and Shame and the Unity of the Mediterranean*. Washington, D.C.: American Anthropological Association, 1987.

Gilmore, David D. "Anthropology of the Mediterranean Area," *Annual Review in Anthropology* 11 (1982), 175–205.

Hsu, Francis L.K. "American Core Value and National Character," pp. 241–262 in F. Hsu, *Psychological Anthropology*. Cambridge: Schenkman Publishing Co., 1972.

Malina, Bruce J., and John J. Pilch, eds. *Dictionary of New Testament Values*. Peabody, MA.: Hendrickson Press, 1991.

Miller, Alice. *For Your Own Good: Hidden Cruelty in Child-rearing and the Roots of Violence*. New York: Farrar, Straus and Giroux, 1983.

Pilch, John J. "Marian Devotion and Wellness Spirituality," *Biblical Theology Bulletin* 20 (1990), 85–94.

Pilch, John J. *Wellness Spirituality*. New York: Crossroad, 1985.

Pilch, John J. *Wellness: Your Invitation to Full Life*. Minneapolis: Winston, 1981.

Resources

The two basic resources for this Bible-study program are (1) a Bible and (2) this workbook.

Any Bible translated from the original languages is recommended. It would be especially helpful if the Bible contains cross-references, notes, maps, and other study aids.

For further information about Bible translations consult:

John J. Pilch, *Selecting a Bible Translation,* Collegeville, MN.: The Liturgical Press, 1987.

Paulist Press publishes two excellent handbooks which can readily serve as supplements to this present Bible-study program for those who have the time and may be interested:

Lawrence Boadt, C.S.P., *Reading the Old Testament: An Introduction.* Paulist Press, 1984.

Pheme Perkins, *Reading the New Testament.* Paulist Press, 1985.

Additional helpful information can be found in the following highly recommended books located in many public and parish libraries:

The Collegeville Bible Commentary, Dianne Bergant and Robert J Karris, eds. Collegeville, MN.: The Liturgical Press, 1988.

A Catholic commentary by Catholic scholars.

Harper's Bible Commentary, James L. Mays, general editor. San Francisco: Harper and Row, 1988.

An ecumenical commentary by outstanding scholars of various denominations, including Catholics.

Harper's Bible Dictionary, Paul J. Achtemeier, general editor. San Francisco: Harper and Row, 1985.

Insightful and pointed articles on many topics of interest to all Bible readers.

There is much information about Mediterranean culture in atlases of the Bible. Recent publications include the following:

The Harper Atlas of the Bible, James C. Pritchard, editor. San Francisco: Harper & Row, 1987.

Atlas of the Bible, John Rogerson. New York: Facts on File Publications, 1985.

The Zondervan NIV Atlas of the Bible, Carl G. Rasmussen. Grand Rapids, MI.: Zondervan, 1989.

Oxford Bible Atlas, H.G. May, editor. Third Revised Edition, New York: Oxford, 1984.

This last book is also excellent and perhaps the most affordable of those listed for a personal library.